The Joy of
Family Rituals

The Joy of
Family Rituals:
Recipes for Everyday Living

Barbara Biziou

St. Martin's Press ☙ New York

Library of Congress Cataloging-in-Publication Data

Biziou, Barbara.
    The joy of family rituals : recipes for everyday living/
Barbara Biziou.
        p.   cm.
    Includes bibliographical references.
    ISBN 0-312-25328-1
    1. Family. 2. Rites and ceremonies. 3. Special days. I. Title
GT242.B58 2000
794.2—dc21   99-087434

First Edition: April 2000

Book design by Leah Carlson-Stanisic

10 9 8 7 6 5 4 3 2 1

To all those who share joy and appreciation for the blessings
in their lives and who teach them to the children of the world

CONTENTS

ACKNOWLEDGMENTS

MANY PEOPLE contributed their time and stories to this book. There are too many to acknowledge individually so I would like to thank all those who opened their hearts and shared their stories with me and made this book possible.

Special thanks to Melinda Blau for shaping my ideas and making my words a practical reality.

To my agent, Eileen Cope at Lowenstein & Associates, for encouraging me to write a second book. And to all the people at Golden Books and St. Martin's Press who believe that family rituals are essential to creating a healthy society, especially Lara Asher, my brilliant editor, Kevin Flynn for his enthusiasm and energy, and the fabulous art and production department for this beautiful book.

My family, spiritual sisters and brothers who know the content of this book through experience, helped me to shape the rituals that mark our extended family life. Everyone who has participated in a ritual with me has added his or her own creative expression to this completed project.

I am deeply grateful to my son Jourdan, my brother Mark, and my mother Diana for their unconditional love and support. And a thanks to Herman for making my mother happy.

To my "Brugh sisters"—thank you for gently pushing me to go beyond my self-imposed limitations. I have relied on the talent and inspiration of many of my friends, especially my "goddess sisters," who generously shared their resources—particularly Laurie Sue Brockway.

Warm thanks to all of the incredibly busy professionals who took the time to let me pick their brains about the importance of family rituals. . . . Pamela Abrams, Susan Lapinsky, Dr. Ron Taffel, Ariel Gore, Susan Frankel, Peter Bayles and all the "Stay at Home Dads," Connie Miller (F.E.M.A.L.E.), Don Campbell, Debra Roth, Miriam Dyack, and Susan Mary Hellerer.

Michael Owen Schwager is proof that a warm heart and a brilliant mind go hand in hand. His dedication to promoting the importance of rituals and my work goes unparalleled.

To Sandi Levine and Ralph White at the New York Open Center for their dedication to quality and making a sacred space available in New York City.

Without my friends, students, and clients, this book would never exist. Thank you for holding the energy for me and reminding me to rest and renew.

Also, special thanks to Nancy Walsh for her breathing techniques, loving heart, and sharp mind. My gratitude as well to Christa Savino, who has kept my office running smoothly. Both women have midwifed this project and have allowed me the time to go in and put on paper what I wanted to share.

Special acknowledgment to all those who have been my teachers and mentors and to all those who hold circles and rituals around the world. I have learned much from all of you.

INTRODUCTION

Why Family *Rituals?*

LONG AGO, I learned the importance of doing family rituals. When my son Jourdan was born, I lived in California. My family of origin (my parents, siblings, and entire extended family) was still in New York, so I found it necessary to redefine "family." I developed a network of close friends on whom I could rely not only for emergencies but also for emotional sustenance on holidays and important occasions. My friends Julia and Michael were "Aunt Julia" and "Uncle Michael" to Jourdan. We began to create our own traditions, which Jourdan looked forward to—they anchored him, especially after his father and I separated.

As a single mother, I had to create new rituals as well. Instead of celebrating Father's Day, which was hard on our family, we made it "Grandfather's Day" and focused on *my* father. Though we lived thousands of miles from my dad, we used the day to create homemade cards and gifts for him. Afterward, we always did

something together that the two of us enjoyed, such as visiting an arcade.

As a young child, Jourdan also had a hard time with change, perhaps because of the upheaval emanating from my divorce when he was four and the subsequent absence of a dad in his life. However, whenever he started a new grade, transferred to a different school, or attended sleep-away camp, I always made special time for the two of us, taking steps that helped him acclimate to the transition. We talked about his feelings rather than hurrying him, and I asked what would make the new situation easier. Although the articles changed as he got older—a treasured teddy bear, a familiar lunch box, a beaten-up backpack—I made sure that he took something old and familiar with him into the unknown. Because pizza was his favorite food, we invariably used it to commemorate the firsts in his life. And whenever I visited him at camp, and later at boarding school, I made a point of going to the same restaurants every time—for pizza, of course.

I didn't have the consciousness then that I do now. Honestly, I didn't even think of those events as rituals. But I realize in retrospect that celebrating with pizza gave Jourdan a sense of constancy. That he could depend on those rituals made the going much smoother.

Jourdan is now a young man in his late twenties, and I look back on our holidays, our separations, our birthdays, and I see that we have marked the passage of time with our rituals. I also see ways in which I could have done even more. For example, instead of making Father's Day something entirely different, I could have called upon several of my male friends, who had become surrogate dads to Jourdan, to join us in creating a ritual that would have at least connected my son with the spirit of a father figure.

To this day, Jourdan and I use ritual to transform ordinary moments into sacred time, and to continue to improve our relationship. If we are having a difficult time or one of us needs to make a transition, we assuage our fears and ease each new passage through ritual. When he got his first car and planned to make his first solo cross-country trip, we did a blessing ritual on his car, and I gave him a pouch filled with various crystals for safety, wisdom, intuition, and other qualities he'd need on the road. More recently, when he moved into his own apartment, we per-

formed my two-part Moving ritual (page 155). The first part involved Jourdan's going through his possessions, deciding what he wanted to throw away, give to someone else, or keep for his new life as an independent young man. It was a wrenching experience for him to say good-bye to his childhood, but very cleansing nonetheless. At his new apartment, I sprinkled salt in the doorway to purify the space, hung a mezuzah in the door frame for protection, and friends came over bearing other symbolic gifts to ensure his happiness and security.

By now, everyone in our family has come to depend upon ritual to ease transitions and to maintain connections. As I describe in greater detail on page 107, shortly after our father died, my brother Mark began hosting an annual family reunion—a weekend at his home in Vermont. Unlike some family gatherings, in which the conversation never rises above the level of small talk, people really share about their lives. They talk about things that have been hard for them during the past year, their hopes and dreams. And every year the event has grown larger, with the definition of our family extending to include my mother's best friend, who comes all the way from Florida, and my father's older brother's best friend and his wife, now in their nineties, who make the six-hour drive from New York City just to be there. They're not blood relatives, but we feel connected to them all the same, and we midlife "youngsters" love to hear their childhood stories, because they help us understand where we came from.

In most respects, my family is no different from yours. We're all searching for a foothold in the past, and for peace and meaning in the chaos of modern life. We all want to give our children a place of refuge and a sense of predictability. We all wish to make the difficult times easier and the unknown feel safer. Rituals have served these functions for ancient cultures; and rituals can now do the same for us, too.

Why Do Parents Feel the Need for Ritual Now?

While I was completing my first book, *The Joy of Ritual,* I began to notice a heartening and important trend: Parents have become increasingly interested in making rituals a natural part of their family life. I've had this confirmed in the questions people ask about my work. Some parents, wanting to share the experience with their children, wonder if it's okay to bring them to my workshops or to particular rituals I perform throughout the year, such as solstice celebrations or my Halloween ritual, in which we honor our ancestors. Other mothers and fathers ask if I'll teach them how to do rituals with kids; some even invite me into their homes.

In the last year alone, I've begun to receive more and more invitations to do family rituals—not only weddings and baby namings, but also *re*marriage rituals to welcome a new stepmother into the family. Of late, I've had parents who want me to help them create ceremonies that deal with difficult family issues, such as death and divorce. Dorothy,* whose last child was going off to college, asked if I might suggest an "empty nest" ritual that she could do with her daughter. Peter, who had been his toddler's primary caretaker, requested a ceremony that could ease both their feelings of separation on the first day of preschool. The Davis family asked me to help them come up with something to help them get through their grief over Fluffy, their nine-year-old cocker spaniel, who had been fatally hit by a car.

Parents also inquire about creating new kinds of family holidays. For example, Sam, whose wife had recently died, wondered what he might do with the children to make Mother's Day easier. Lenny and Diane, parents of different faiths, wanted to create traditions that honored both sides of the family. And many of the parents and grandparents I talk with are simply interested in using ritual to achieve what seems to me the most

---

*All names in this book have been changed as much as possible, as well as certain identifying details. For simplicity, the pronouns "he" and "she" are alternated.

important challenge facing families today: maintaining a strong sense of connection, with each other, with the community, and with God (or some other spiritual Being).

I must say, parents' interest in ritual doesn't come as a great surprise to me. We are living in times that beg for tradition and ceremonies to make us feel safe and grounded and, at the same time, keep us connected to a spiritual center. Today's families are facing problems and new family configurations that preceding generations never had to think about—coparenting with an ex, being a single parent or a stepparent, raising foster children or half siblings, or adopting children from other cultures. We are rewriting the rules and redefining the forms that families can take. Where there are no guidelines, we have to create them.

Parents today are also more isolated than ever. Many work outside the home and are on busy, tight schedules—as are their children. The complexities of daily living, not to mention a shortage of quality time, weigh heavily on everyone. But rituals can keep a family together. Regular and steady, they are the cement that today's kids need to feel secure. Indeed, after psychologists Steven and Sybil Wolin conducted a series of studies on dysfunctional families, they concluded that rituals act as a buffer against problems.

Likewise, family therapist Ron Taffel advises that parents can engender respect and forge connection with their children "by creating predictable routines and rituals." He refers to birthday and anniversary celebrations, intergenerational family gatherings, or any kind of tradition, such as storytelling, that makes family history come to life. He also defines as "ritual" the ordinary, recurring routines we share with our children—stories at bedtime, the drive or walk to school, weekly board games, even Saturday chores. The constancy of these mundane occurrences gives children a sense of stability. In fact, when he asked kids from nursery school through sixth grade, "What is your favorite thing to do?" 80 percent—four out of five—cited everyday rituals with their parents. Taffel advises, "Rituals should continue as long as people live—and in the best families, I've found that they do."

About This Book

Rituals are a natural part of my family's life. And my lectures, tapes, and workshops have inspired thousands of other parents to bring ritual into their families' lives. My intention here is to share my "recipes" with you—to teach you how and when to use ritual as a practical, simple tool to help you connect, reflect, cope with problems, gain insights, heighten your intuition, and discover elements of the Sacred. Included are rituals for even the most mundane occurrences—like eating a meal or taking a bath. As I explain in Chapter 1, almost anything can be a ritual. What's important is not the act so much as the intention: *to develop and maintain a habit of mindfulness, whether around everyday experiences or special occasions.*

The format of this book resembles a cookbook. The first chapter offers an overview of process and practice. I explain what rituals are and the ways they create possibilities to bring you into a sacred space and remind you of who you truly are and of your connection to the universe. Chapter 2 is a tour of the kitchen, in which I talk about working with different types of ingredients when you're cooking up a ritual. Chapter 3 reminds you of the resources and practices within yourself—the raw materials, as I call them. The remaining six chapters focus on the rituals themselves, from the ordinary and everyday to holidays and special family days, as well as rituals that help you deal with feelings and shepherd your family through change. For each occasion, I introduce the concept, offering a bit of cultural context and history as a backdrop, as well as the intention of the ritual, its timing, the ingredients, the recipe, and, when applicable, the follow-up steps. Finally, I offer one or more real-life examples, which I call a "Ritual Reality," to show you how other families have used my recipe or created variations of their own.

I believe that these recipes, which represent the most common uses of ritual, will enrich and enliven your everyday family life while, quite literally, feeding your soul. However, I can't predict the specific events or concerns that may arise in your life, so you may want to come up with some recipes tailored to your own circumstances and needs. Use my ideas for inspiration, and then use your imagination to create rituals that fulfill your own needs. Allow your intention to steer you toward a course that's right for you.

The more you understand what rituals are and how they can enrich and anchor your family, the more you will want to incorporate them into your everyday life, as well as your special moments together. As you will learn in the next chapter, anything can become a ritual, as long as your intention is clear, and you set aside the sacred time and space. All you have to do is allow the light of the universe to shine into your heart.

1. What *Is* Ritual?

UNDOUBTEDLY, you have had moments such as these in your family life: You arrive home after a day at the office, and your toddler flies into your arms, saying, "Up!" You give her a big squeeze and a kiss. Before bedtime, you read to your older child. Thursday night, you order pizza; Sunday mornings, you make French toast. Every spring, you go through your closets and get rid of clothes you haven't worn in a while. When the holiday season rolls around, you always ask your children to give toys to the homeless, you hunt for that carton of homemade tree ornaments, and you make the same pudding your grandmother made when you were a child.

Most of us participate regularly in rituals without realizing it. You may not think that a daily trip to the playground or a family breakfast qualifies as a ritual, but it does. I call them *unconscious* rituals. Sadly, while we do these things often and may even look forward to them as part of our routine, we don't recognize their significance in our lives.

In other instances, we may partake in celebrations, such as birthdays, anniversaries, holidays, even religious rites, but give little or no thought to their deeper meaning or to their sacred connection to the past. For many of us, these traditions have become what I call *rote* rituals. We may throw parties to commemorate an event or participate by attending services and ceremonies rooted in family heritage. However, we do so because that's the way things have always been done—not necessarily because they mean something to us on a personal level.

Many of the rituals of my childhood, and probably yours, were rote rituals. I never questioned them, and I suspect you didn't either. I did them because I was expected to. I did them without thinking of the deeper spiritual meaning of the practice. I did them not realizing that each of these time-honored rites connected me to my past. Looking back, I can see that although I enjoyed many of these traditions, the spirit at the heart of each ritual seemed to be missing. I sensed that there must be a deeper meaning to those rituals, and I longed to discover it.

What Rituals Do for Us

As it turns out, I wasn't alone. Other people have felt that something is missing in their lives, too. We all long to return to the time when a wedding truly celebrated a rite of passage, when the naming of a child was a sacred event, not simply the act of picking out a good name from a baby book, and when the lighting of candles signified a real desire to illuminate—to bring virtue, healing, and the presence of God into our homes. We hunger for both community and communion, the feelings found in the *conscious* practice of rituals. They not only help us make sense of the world and where we fit into it but they also expand our awareness and connect us to the great mystery of life. In fact, the very word *ritual,* derived from an Indo-European root, means "to fit together." Every ritual conveys an act in which we literally join the metaphysical with the physical. It is a means of calling Spirit into our material lives.

As Thomas Moore reminds us in *Care of the Soul,* "Rituals maintain the world's holiness. Knowing that everything we do, no matter how simple, has a halo of imagination around it and

can serve the soul, enriches life and makes the things around us more precious, more worthy of our protection and care."

While there are many types of rituals, in each case you create a smaller symbolic event to symbolize a larger event. Hence, rituals include any kind of *rite* (for example, a christening), *ceremony* (a wedding), *tradition* (hanging stockings), *service* (any action performed in worship, such as the Hindu *puja,* which includes offering flowers to the guru), *liturgy* (the Catholic Mass), honoring a *spiritual object* (a Tibetan prayer flag) or *mantra* (a sound, like "om," uttered repeatedly), and even *etiquette* (a handshake, saying "hello" or "thank you"). A ritual is similar to *prayer* as well, in the sense that it encourages us to enter into a state of grace. In fact, one of the deepest instincts of human beings is to find spirituality.

Rituals can be used for many purposes: connecting with members of your family and bringing new people into the family, ushering in a new life stage, dealing with first-time events and transitions, healing, enhancing creativity, even acknowledging daily routines. They can take seconds or hours. They can be simple or complex, traditional or created in the moment to meet a specific need. And they can be performed with one or two family members or with your entire extended clan. By using rituals, we help ourselves and our children make better sense of the world.

Many ancient cultures have used rituals to strengthen their family ties and to deepen their relationships. For example, in South America it is common practice for a mother or grandmother to bless each person as he or she leaves the house in the morning, with the intention of strengthening the family bond as well as each family member's connection to Spirit. In Mediterranean cultures, as in Italy and Spain, it's customary for everyone to come home for lunch. Dad leaves work, the children get a break from school, and everyone, even grandparents, takes part in a midday family meal.

Rituals can mark everyday moments or significant times; they can ease us through transitions and, especially in times of rapid change, bring structure and stability into family life. Rituals enable families to connect to something larger than their individual selves, to evoke the sense of a Higher Force and, at the same time, be guided in day-to-day affairs. They allow us to bring a sacred feeling even to ordinary family moments, like meals and bedtimes, transforming them into times of quiet reflection and connection. Perhaps most important, family traditions and rites help establish a common spiritual ground on which bonds can be forged—bonds that transcend age, gender, and individual interests. Indeed, a strong spiritual life can help a family achieve harmony even when there are unusual differences. As Annie, a mother who had adopted eight children from different countries, told me, "Our family rituals bridge the gaps between cultures. They give us an even playing field."

The Elements of a Ritual

All rituals—everyday or special-event rituals—have five key elements that work together to create a basic ritual recipe.

Intention—This is the *purpose* of a ritual. You have breakfast with the children with the intention of helping everyone set goals for the day. Or, you plan a meaningful birthday ritual for your daughter's sweet sixteen—as opposed to just throwing a party—with the intention of reviewing her life and having her guests express how special she is. What is important is that your intention is pure and that you're sincere.

Sequence—Every ritual has a clear beginning and end. You start with an act, like meditation or lighting a candle, to herald the beginning. At the end, you have some form of closure, usually a moment of quiet reflection, that acknowledges the experience.

Sacred Space—Because rituals evoke a change of consciousness, they need to take place outside of ordinary life. This isn't as difficult to achieve as it sounds. First of all, *intention* and a clear *beginning* contribute to creating a sacred space. Therefore, you can transform your everyday environment into ritual space by simply inhaling a few deep breaths or by moving your child's toys aside to create a sacred area in the living room. Of course, you can also go to greater lengths—for instance, by building an altar or making a fire.

۵ **Ingredients**—Many rituals employ candles, colors, scents, food, music, crystals, objects, animals, even physical acts as symbolic elements. I have devoted all of Chapter 2 to the wide variety of ingredients available in your "ritual kitchen," as I call it, many of which are items, such as toy figures and stuffed animals, crayons and construction paper, our children enjoy using.

۵ **Personal Meaning**—Although this book is chock full of suggestions, what works for one family or person may not work for another. Certainly, rituals done for a thousand years have a power of their own, and it's important to follow specific steps in re-creating them. But if a ritual has no meaning for you, that power will be lost. It has to signify something in *your* heart to reach *you*. When daily habits become important to us,

they take on an almost sacred meaning. Therefore, creating your own personal rituals can have the most power.

You'll be surprised by how easily you can turn an everyday occasion into a ritual. Notice how Mr. Rogers always begins his TV show by changing his shoes and putting on a comfortable sweater. That simple act notes his *intention*—to relax and enjoy the time with his viewers—and also signals *the beginning*. At the end of the show, he reverses the process, letting everyone know that it's *the end*.

You can bring the same consciousness to the ordinary events that transpire in your own home. For example, you might already take your child to the park at the same time every day. You bring certain snacks, the dog comes along, and your child always carries her favorite doll. But you don't really *think* about the purpose of your trip—other than seeing it as a good way to give your child a breath of fresh air and both of you some exercise. Suppose instead, that you intend to make your daily park trip a time of connection, so that each moment with your child will affirm your love and foster a sense of security. Suppose that you now think about the sequence. Pay close attention to the beginning—be conscious of your actions as you make snacks and get your child's coat on. Then say out loud, "Time for our park adventure!" In this way, you mark the start of your ritual.

On the way to the park, even with a very young child, you can recite your intention: "Sarah and Mommy are going to have fun at the park. This is our special time together." Even if Sarah doesn't understand the words at first, I guarantee you that she'll feel the meaning. At the park, instead of just giving Sarah her snack, if you take a moment to say grace, to express thanks for the beautiful day, and to enjoy the snack together, the mundane moment is elevated to a spiritual experience. And, after every visit, instead of just coming into the house and getting busy with chores, mark the end of your ritual. Remove your shoes, have a drink of water (or juice) to cleanse your system, and give the dog a biscuit in appreciation for accompanying you. Thus, the usual trip to the park becomes a ritual of togetherness.

The same holds true of special occasion rituals, such as weddings, baby showers, or child-naming ceremonies. Instead of just creating the guest list and planning the menu, slow down and realize that you're participating in a time-honored tradition that connects you to your past and to your family. Concentrate on your intention—to commemorate an important rite of passage—and you will get, and give, a deeper meaning and a greater sense of connectedness from each occasion. The same is true when you are invited to an event. Instead of just buying a present, put yourself into a sacred space, and let your intuition guide you toward a meaningful gift that honors the celebrant.

Why Rituals Work

Rituals have great power and influence over our minds. Dr. W. Brugh Joy, a physician who teaches workshops on the mind-body-spirit connection as well as the connections between Eastern and Western thought, explains, "There's a part of your psyche that doesn't know the difference between a ritual as opposed to an actual event." Hence, if you have shown your child how to take a ritual bath with the intention of relaxation, there will be a part of him that thinks the bath will ease his tension and loosen his muscles and therefore he can now begin anew. Or, if you teach your children to meditate in the morning with the intention of renewal, you all will feel more energetic, insightful, and clear, because each of you has told your brains to expect these changes.

As a family, you can do a ritual to honor a deceased grandparent or even a pet, and you will all feel more connected to the loved one even though he or she is not actually there with you. Even young children grasp this concept. I know a seven-year-old disabled boy who recently went to synagogue with his mother on Yom Kippur. During a part of the service in which people were allowed to share about loved ones who had passed away, he stood up and said, "God Bless you, Grandpa. I love you." He still missed the old man, who died two years earlier, but feeling he could "talk" to him gave the boy comfort.

Your brain cannot distinguish the intensity of meanings. For example, if you do ten sit-ups in the morning or fifty, your brain doesn't know the difference; all it knows is that your intention is to be fit and healthy. Likewise, when you participate in a ritual, in essence you are telling your brain that you already have completed whatever you're enacting symbolically. Visualization techniques work for the same reason. In short, rituals are consciously structured acts intended to influence our subconscious mind. In this way, they strengthen our resolve to work toward achieving what we desire.

Recently, I helped my friend Susan deal with an unexpected change in her family. She had known for several months that her seventy-nine-year-old father, a recent widower living in a retirement village in Miami, had begun seeing Isabelle, a woman a few years his junior. The two of them had gone out to dinner, played Bingo, even paired up at a dance, and Susan was delighted to hear the new energy in her father's voice. But when Dad announced to her that he and his "lady" were planning to set up house together, Susan was appalled. "It all seemed so innocent and sweet until now. I never imagined it coming to *this,*" she admitted.

The new living arrangement was hard on Susan and her older brother both because it made them feel disloyal to their mother and also because it forced them to see their dad in a new light—an aging Romeo! Like it or not, though, Susan knew she not only had to get used to the idea of her father being part of a couple, she had to embrace it. She asked for my help, and I told her about my ritual for Welcoming a New Family Member (page 166). Because she feared that two septuagenarians might be put off by a Japanese tea ceremony, she adapted the idea of my ritual to a more appropriate format. I agreed; in planning a ritual, it's important to gauge what others will find palatable. Susan knew her dad didn't like anyone making a fuss over him. So Susan and her brother Ivan simply told their dad they were coming to Miami to take Isabelle and him out to a special dinner.

Before the meal, Ivan recited a poem he'd written, celebrating Dad and Isabelle. Susan gave them his and hers champagne goblets, and a picture frame inscribed with their names. It was a simple ceremony, but afterward everyone felt a lot less like strangers and more like family. Dad was delighted because deep down, even though he didn't need his adult children's approval, he wanted it. And Susan discovered that she really liked Isabelle. "I thought I'd resent her for not being my mother, but in spite of myself, I found it was really easy to be her friend. And now I don't have to worry about Dad being alone."

Rituals invariably change the dynamics of a situation. Whether you or your children are stymied by a project, paralyzed by fear, or burdened by sadness, a ritual that has meaning can help shift everyone's consciousness, reduce the tension, and ease difficult passages. For example, when Dana, a psychotherapist who lives in San Francisco, stopped nursing her then three-and-a-half-year-old daughter Rachel, she designed a ritual to commemorate that important transition. She invited extended family and friends to share the occasion. "I sent out invitations with a logo I designed—a picture of breasts and wings," Dana explained in an E-mail to me. "I also made a cake with the same logo on it and wrote 'Goodbye to nursing' on top. The party was festive and sad at the same time—a real passing of something important." Dana also made a small book for Rachel, including photographs of the two of them, as well as of friends, and a story about her giving up nursing, her feelings about the loss, and ways she could now find comfort and closeness when she needed it. "That seemed to help a lot in the weeks and months that followed," recalls Dana. "Rachael kept the book on her shelves and looked at the pictures the first year whenever she was thinking about nursing."

A year later, when Rachel was ready to give up her pacifier, Dana did another ritual with her, again inviting everyone to share the moment. To signify Rachel's "letting go," Mom and her friends tied a pacifier to a helium balloon in the backyard and let it fly away. This time, the cake had miniature pacifiers all over it. And that night, after all the guests had gone, Dana told Rachel to put her pacifier under her pillow for the "Passie Fairy," who left her little gifts. "This, too, was a hard passing," admits Dana, "but it was greatly assisted by the ritual."

Rituals aren't magic but they can certainly *seem* magical. Whether they're done in the privacy of your home or backyard, in the sanctity of a church or temple, or in a hall packed with a thousand people, rituals can ease a transition, inspire a new approach to an old problem, help heal the wounds of a bad relationship, or bond a new family together. I get calls every day from former students who are amazed at the difference after only a few weeks of performing a particular ritual. As one woman told me, "I realize that I'm giving myself a different message, and as a result, my life is going in a new direction."

There's another reason rituals work: *They slow us down.* The Buddhists have a concept called "mindfulness" that embodies the idea of paying attention to the here-and-now. As we slow down, we gain a new perspective on our life and are better able to deal with its ups and downs. So many of us spend time reliving the past or worrying about the future that we wind up missing out on (or ruining) the present. We can change such unhealthy patterns, learning to stay centered in the present and, at the same time, honor the past. When, in turn, we teach these skills to our children, we prepare them to cope and help them consciously envision their future in a positive, directed way.

Children and Rituals

Rituals are particularly wonderful for families, because they bring adults and children together in a sacred space. If we take the time to stop and bless what we have—our loved ones, our food, our home—and to honor the seasons of change, both within the family and on the planet, we can learn to appreciate each moment and gain happiness from living in the fullness of the present. By using rituals, we help ourselves and our children make better sense of the world. They begin to regard even the mundane—a bath or a family dinner—as sacred moments of connection and togetherness.

When I travel to other countries, I'm often struck by the routine inclusion of children in ceremonies and rites. Parents don't even think to leave the kids home with baby-sitters; they don't consider them an intrusion. Rather, they teach them to participate. It's no accident that many of the family rituals I suggest in these pages are based on those of other countries or borrowed from ancient rituals or native cultures that haven't been as affected by progress and industrialization as we have. In those societies, people use rituals to honor the passage of seasons, mark important occasions, and find solace and guidance through times of uncertainty. Just as important, such rites are also a way of introducing their young people to the customs of the tribe and of teaching them the basic skills and knowledge they need to survive.

There was a time in our history, prior to the Industrial Revolution, when this happened naturally in our culture, too. Children and adults worked side by side on the farm or in cottage industries that were run out of people's homes. In those days, says Tom Cowan, author of *Shamanism,* "childhood" wasn't even recognized as a separate stage of life. Unlike the adult/child differences we see today in style of clothing, activities, playthings, even expectations, Cowan points out, "children were not separated from adult experiences and segregated into environments composed primarily of children their own age. . . ." Children were told their family history by the elders of the community; through these stories, they also learned about puberty, reproduction, and the needs of the family for sustenance. As a result, they were more intimately connected to their ancestors, to their tribes, and to the natural cycles of life, from birth to death.

The rituals of olden days helped adults *and*

children understand their rightful place in the cosmic scheme of things. In contrast, today's children often see *themselves* as the center of the universe. We take our kids to child-focused activities and tend to shield them from many of the realities of life. We don't want them to worry about adult concerns. We have few rites of passage, and rarely do elders sit around telling stories to children. In this way, we unwittingly contribute to the separation between children and adults. As Judith Rich Harris points out in *The Nurture Assumption,* rather than viewing parents and elders as resources, many children today look to their peers for guidance.

Don't worry. Parents needn't throw their hands up in desperation. Rituals may not be the only antidote to the parent/child chasm, but they certainly make a difference in family life. They encourage children to focus on the adults in their environment and listen to their wisdom. Your children will enjoy rituals, look forward to them, learn from them, and feel comforted and grounded by their consistency. Breakfast can become a time when they learn to quiet their mind before a busy day. At night, saying prayers, reading a book, or doing a relaxation ritual helps them ease into bedtime. Being part of a ceremony to welcome new family members concretely broadens the boundaries of the family.

Recurrent traditions and special ceremonies not only teach children about life and help them feel more connected to adults, they also help make kids aware of the bigger picture. Through ritual, children begin to see where they fit into the immediate family, how they are connected to the extended family and to the generations that came before them, and where they are in the family of humankind.

As I explain in the next chapter, in planning rituals for your family, you will want to consider what is developmentally appropriate for your child or children. You'll probably have to experiment a bit at first. Still, you'll find that most rituals can be adapted for very young children. Even when kids don't understand what's going on, they can *feel* that it's something special and sacred. Many parents have been amazed at their toddlers' unusually long attention spans and patience during rituals. My hunch is that children "get" spirituality more easily than adults. They're born open to it, and they haven't yet built up the skepticism or the defenses that we adults have learned. In the midst of a sacred moment, they can sense that something important is transpiring, and they are often mesmerized by the process.

As your children grow and change, so might your traditions. It's important to note, too, that your family rituals may transform over time, not only because of change within your family—children getting older, relocation, new interests and pursuits—but also because of cultural shifts.

For example, fifty years ago, Jewish girls had no rite of passage comparable to their brothers' Bar Mitzvah; today many girls celebrate Bat Mitzvah. Likewise, a decade back, people meditated but few talked about it—it certainly wasn't a mainstream practice. Now many do, among them parents, who have started teaching and involving their kids at younger and younger ages.

In researching this book, I have heard wonderful stories about family rituals. Of course, many parents already conduct rituals; they consider bedtime stories, weekend outings, and family dinners sacred, and they schedule these moments the way they do their business appointments. These parents report that if, by chance, they forget to do these familiar rituals, their children are quick to remind them. Many families have created unique traditions, as different from one another as their families are. You will meet many of them in the Ritual Realities I offer following each recipe.

Sarah, for instance, does karate with her son; they take classes at the same *dojo* but in different rooms, and at a specific time each night, they practice together. Gregory plays a weekly game of golf with his daughter. Claire, who adopted a virtual United Nations of children, celebrates a winter holiday that honors each child's roots. And Joanne has a regular sleep-over date with her nine-year-old nephew Seth. She also takes him out once a month for dinner, a tradition she started when Seth's father—Joanne's brother—died several years ago. Both of them have come to depend on, and look forward to, their simple ritual.

I have seen children brought up on ritual, and it *does* make a difference. These kids have a sense of spirituality from a very early age; rituals have given them a number of ways to develop a personal relationship with the Divine. They also feel a connection to the earth, have a deep regard for all of its creatures, and are aware of the cycles of life. Especially if you start when your children are young, family rituals help keep the lines of communication open as well. And the structure and predictability help kids feel secure. The way I see it, ritual is surely a gift that keeps giving.

2. Tools of the Trade:

Finding Your Way Around the Ritual Kitchen

ALL GOOD COOKS need to learn their way around the kitchen—how to use various utensils and appliances, as well as understand the specific properties of ingredients—and what their effect will be when added to a recipe. And certainly, a true chef must have a general idea of the entire process: how to get started, what to do if a particular ingredient is not available, and how to know when the dish is finished. The same process applies to rituals. Before you serve up some of these wonderful delicacies to your family, you'll need to acquaint yourself with the ritual kitchen.

What's in Your Pantry?

Believe it or not, you already have at home many of the necessary ingredients for creating rituals—in your closets, cabinets, and in the natural environment. Let me explain: The ingredients of rituals—symbolic objects, colors, aromas, tex-

tures, movements, and sounds—all carry meaning. Some, used for centuries by cultures around the world, have evolved into *universal symbols* with a power of their own. For example, a circle is universally recognized as a symbol for wholeness; an egg represents life and rebirth. Other ingredients that you choose for your rituals—a framed photo of your grandmother or a scent that reminds your children of a happy occasion—have *personal* meaning. People often develop rituals based on accessible materials, immediate climate, and living conditions; Hawaiians tend to use the lush flora and ocean surrounding them, while city dwellers gravitate toward indoor rituals.

Here I will introduce you to the basic provisions in my ritual pantry; and in Chapter 3, we'll talk about specific ways to use them. I describe the meaning of each ingredient according to its most common *Western* interpretation. In our culture, red symbolizes passion, energy, and creation; not many American brides would wear red to their weddings as Chinese brides do! In any case, remember that the most important meaning is the one *you* attach.

Also, keep in mind that these are only guidelines to get you started. Some of the ingredients may be hard to find if you live in a small town, so I've included (on pages 174–175) a list of mail-order companies where you can purchase oils, incense, and special music. However, feel free to improvise at any time by using substitutes that you find locally. As you gain confidence, you'll become more creative with your ingredients—just like any good cook.

You also might want to have your children help you make items needed for rituals, such as candles and simple instruments. As a family project, you might grow flowers or herbs in a garden or in pots on the windowsill. Indeed, one of the benefits of family rituals is that they encourage children to engage in old-fashioned play, which involves drawing, painting, puppet-making. Sadly, in many homes children rarely engage in such arts and crafts projects. Instead, they are engrossed in media-inspired toys and electronic gadgetry; even their fantasies are often based on TV or movie plots. Getting your family involved in rituals won't drown out the constant noise of the kiddie culture, but at least it will inspire your kids to use their own imaginations.

Candles

For centuries, candles have been lit to welcome Spirit, and to symbolize a connection to inner light. The act of lighting a candle creates a sense of serenity and holiness that adults and children can carry into the world. To enhance a candle's power, you can choose a particular color (page 13) and/or scent (pages 14–15). Naturally, with small children, you'll want to be cautious when lighting and positioning candles.

Colors

Colors evoke feeling. As Russian abstract painter Wassily Kandinsky said, "Colors directly influence the soul." And children love color. What child is not delighted with a set of crayons or paints? Throughout this book, I suggest appropriate colors to incorporate into your rituals through a particular candle, piece of fabric or garment, colored paper, fruit, flower, leaf, or anything else you choose to use. However, you may have your own interpretation of colors—maybe green reminds you of your mother, who loved wearing it. Likewise, if blue is your child's favorite color, using it in a ritual might feel comforting and help him or her feel included. Honor these personal associations by adapting them for your own rituals.

❧ COLORS ❧

Black: release, the unknown
Blue: clarity, communication, peace, trust, creativity, innovation
Brown: earth, grounding, the ability to produce
Gold: prosperity, strength, courage, self-confidence, the solar principle, the masculine
Green: healing, balance, prosperity, harmony, generosity
Indigo: intuition, trust, feelings, clarity, vision, fearlessness
Maroon: sensuality
Orange: joy, sexuality, vitality, spontaneity, optimism, playfulness
Pink: love, compassion
Purple: spirituality, inspiration, leadership
Red: passion, energy, creation, stamina
Silver: wisdom, fertility, nourishment, growth, the lunar principle, the feminine
Turquoise: clarity, peace
White: purity, universal color
Yellow: power, manifestation, willpower, the intellect, logical thinking

Scents

For centuries, scents have been used in ritual. The ancients knew that the aroma of plants and essential oils could create change in their lives. Moving into modern times, the word "aromatherapy" was first used in the 1920s, to describe the healing and rejuvenating uses of essential oils or plant essences for therapeutic purposes. Scientific research has since confirmed that scents alone have the power to alter one's state of mind. The reason is simple: Of all five senses, only smell travels directly to the brain. The scent of chalk can instantly conjure images of a favorite teacher; inhaling ocean air may bring back memories of a family vacation.

Even more important, our sense of smell is linked to our emotions. The smell of hot chocolate can remind your child of an ice skating outing; if he had a great time, the aroma will fill him with happiness; if he fell on the ice and bruised himself repeatedly that day, the memories evoked by that aroma might put him in a bad mood. Therefore, it's best to experiment with different scents; try to delight your senses, but always choose those that have the most positive meaning. Doing a relaxation ritual with lavender oil, for example, would be counterproductive if the aroma brings back negative memories of an aunt who wears lavender perfume and frightens your child!

Herbs, spices, and flowers can be found in the form of incense, essential oils, or in their natural state. I recommend using only natural oils because synthetic oils don't carry the same vibration. Scott Cunningham explains in his book, *Magical Aromatherapy,* "Essential oils are concentrated plant energies, therefore essential oils are powerful reservoirs of natural energies." However, these oils are also typically very strong; use them sparingly. For herbs and flowers, look in your local health food store or supermarket, or grow them in your family garden. To retain freshness, these types of ingredients should be stored away from heat, light, and moisture.

Sometimes, adults and children are allergic to a fragrance or herb, so be careful. If you know of specific allergies, avoid those scents. Or, before performing a ritual, do a little aroma test, by dabbing a bit of oil on a cotton ball and allowing everyone to smell it. Pregnant women should also exercise extreme care. Maggie Tisserand, author of *Aromatherapy for Women,* suggests avoiding certain essential oils, among them those extracted from cinnamon bark, basil, pennyroyal, myrrh, sage, and thyme. (Other good sources of information regarding sensitivities to various scents are Robert Tisserand's *Essential Oil Safety Data Manual* and Scott Cunningham's *Magical Aromatherapy*; see Resources, page 171.)

❧ SCENTS ❧

Basil: clarity, success, prosperity
Bay Leaf: protection
Bergamot: peace, relaxation, sleep, opening heart
Black Pepper: protection, energy, courage
Cedar: connection to the earth, grounding
Chamomile: peace, relaxation
Cinnamon: prosperity
Citrus Oils (lemon, grapefruit, orange, lime): joy, purification, revitalization
Cloves: memory, clarity
Copal (my personal favorite, usually found in resin form): purification
Cypress: comfort (especially for the loss of a loved one), transition
Daffodil: new beginnings, transitions
Dill: mental clarity, sharpening the senses
Eucalyptus: healing, purification, flexibility
Frankincense: spirituality, meditation, releasing fear and anxiety
Freesia: love, peace
Geranium: happiness
Ginger: courage, confidence, creating male sexual desire
Honeysuckle: prosperity, weight loss
Hops: sleep, healing
Iris: love

Jasmine: sexuality, love, facilitating childbirth, clearing obstacles, antidepressant

Juniper: health, vitality, purification, inner strength

Lavender: calming (good for insomnia), cleansing karmic patterns and emotional conflicts, helping access grief

Lemon: health

Lotus Blossoms: unrealized dreams, rebirth

Magnolia: love

Melissa: soothing, brings acceptance, strengthening nerves

Mimosa: dreams

Mint: clarity

Myrrh: spirituality, meditation, healing

Neroli: joy, uplifting, calms charged emotional states

Nutmeg: prosperity, good luck

Parsley: protection

Patchouli: aphrodisiac, reduces frigidity and impotence

Pennyroyal: physical energy, protection

Pepper: courage, energy

Pine: connection to the earth, grounding

Rose: love, compassion, opening the heart, enhancing beauty

Rosemary: positive change, sharpening memory, longevity

Sage: purification, speaking intentions

Sandalwood: relieving anxiety, centering

Spicknard: connection to the earth, grounding

Thyme: courage, health

Tulip: purification

Vanilla: joy, uplifting, relieving depression

Vetivert: connection to the earth, grounding

Ylang-Ylang: happiness, sexual energy

The scents of oils, herbs, flowers, or spices are used in almost every ritual, albeit in different ways, depending on the situation. A baby-naming ritual might call for burning herbs such as copal or sage. For certain other rituals, such as bath or bedtime for young children, it might make more sense to combine the herb or oil with water and put it in a spray bottle. You can release the aroma of essential oils, flowers, herbs, and spices in the following ways:

ᕤ Place the oil on a piece of cotton and inhale.

ᕤ Pour a few drops of oil in a diffuser, which, like an air freshener, will spread the aroma throughout your home. You can buy three different types of diffusers. One is a small bowl into which you mix the herbs or a few drops of oil with some water and a candle beneath the bowl heats the contents. The other two kinds are electric. One has a small fan that releases a mist of scented air. The other has a piece of cardboard that is soaked in the scent like a plug-in air freshener. (Diffusers are available in candle shops, New Age stores, or by mail order; see Sources, page 174.)

    Pour a few drops of oil in a spray bottle filled with water, and spray the fragrant mist around your home.

    Herbs, like basil or sage, can be chopped; spices, like peppercorns or cloves, can be crushed. Place them—with or without oil— in a bowl of warm water. Inhale directly or allow the aroma to infuse the room like potpourri.

    Certain herbs, such as sage, cedar, sweetgrass, and lavender, can be "smudged"—bundled up, tied together, lit at one end, and blown out. The smoldering herbs will permeate the air to purify the space and then can be extinguished by dipping them into a glass of water. (As with candles, be careful with small children.)

Food and Drink

Not only are certain rituals related to meals, such as saying grace or conducting a Passover Seder, but food itself can also be used symbolically. Many cultures offer food on altars, believing that it will give sustenance to the deities. Ancient Egyptians buried their dead with food because they believed that it nurtured the departed spirit. Hindus and Buddhists share this belief, and Hindus often use fruit as an offering. On Rosh Hashanah, the Jewish New Year, an apple, symbolizing nature, is dipped in honey to bring sweetness into the coming year. Native Americans use corn or cornmeal to signify the abundance of a harvest. And when a family moves into a new home, friends often bring bread, sugar, and salt, signifying nourishment, sweetness, and purification.

Of course, many edibles also carry personal meanings. Adults and children often have comfort foods—for example, the healing property of chicken soup is almost universally recognized. Everyone expects cake on his or her birthday. Even at very young ages, children associate chocolate bunnies with Easter, turkey with Thanksgiving, candy canes with Christmas. We can use food to represent where we live, where we came from, and its meaning to us and our loved ones. In fact, many of the rituals I suggest in this book use food as a symbol or end with a feast of your favorite foods and beverages. Before employing a particular food in a ritual involving children, however, always consider your child's tastes and age; young children don't usually enjoy spicy foods. Most important, think not only about what the food signifies, but also what it means on a personal level. Sometimes, simple is best. For example, I often suggest to parents that they use pizza, ice cream, or a favorite kid dish like meatballs and spaghetti to celebrate if that's what their children love most.

ᥨ FOOD AND DRINK ᥨ

Bread: earth, harvest, abundance
Cake: celebration, sweetness
Citrus Fruits: joy, vitality
Corn: earth, harvest, abundance
Eggs: bounty, spiritual renewal, rebirth
Fruit: abundance, health, potential
Grains: earth, harvest, abundance
Grape Juice: celebration, bounty, abundance
Honey, Sugar, Molasses, Chocolate: sweetness
Hot Spices: sexuality, creativity
Ice: frozen emotions
Mangoes: sensuality
Milk: nurturing, sustenance
Oysters: sensuality, hidden beauty
Pomegranate: rebirth, abundance
Popcorn: creativity, new ideas
Rice: earth, harvest, abundance
Salt: purification

Seeds and Sprouts: new potential
Water: emotions, subconscious, source of life, purification
Wine: celebration, bounty, abundance, creation of new life (red wine: feminine power—white wine: masculine power)

Music

Anyone who has ever attended a rock concert or a classical music recital has experienced the transforming power of music. An important aspect of rituals, music helps create or alter a mood, touching your physical, emotional, and spiritual being. Songs with a repeating chorus, chant, or mantra can produce almost trance-like states. Music unites people, as well; when twenty thousand voices sing the national anthem at a ball game, the entire crowd becomes one.

Certain rhythms emulate a heartbeat and their repetition can help adults and children feel more balanced. It is no wonder that drumming is such a universally employed technique in rituals around the world. Don Campbell, author of *The Mozart Effect,* documents the fact that music can slow down and equalize brain waves, boost productivity, strengthen memory and learning, as well as generate a sense of safety and well-being. In a private interview he shared that even fifteen minutes of making music, intoning, or humming can restore health and alleviate stress.

Sound and rhythm enhance almost any ritual, so experiment with different types of music to evoke the mood you wish to create. Help your kids make their own percussion instruments. For a rattle, cut off the top of a dried gourd and fill it with beans or pebbles. Glue the top on and, if you like, paint or decorate it. An old pot easily becomes a "drum," as does an oatmeal carton; and chopsticks or spoons can be drumsticks. Glasses filled with different amounts of water and hit with a chopstick or spoon become xylophones. Tape bells onto paper or plastic plates, and you have tambourines; hit two together, and they're cymbals.

Choose joyful sounds and rhythms for celebrations, calming tones for relaxation rituals, and sacred music for weddings or rites of passage. Use chants and prayers in other languages; you'll be amazed to find that even though none of you understand the words, you'll all experience the *feeling* that the music evokes. And of course you should use family favorites, too—for example, a birthday celebration will mean more to a child when his or her favorite song is played; a memorial ritual becomes more poignant when it includes music that the dearly departed loved to listen to or play.

Crystals

A crystal is an earth element—a mineral or gemstone. Interestingly, your children, who may spend more time outside than you do, might already be familiar with rocks and minerals in your area. If they're not, exploring the properties of crystals helps children learn about nature's wonders and connects them to the earth. Both ancient cultures and modern science have utilized the mysterious qualities of crystals, which have the ability to receive and transmit energy. Egyptians, Australian aboriginals, and Native Americans used them in healing rituals, and they now serve as the cornerstone of digital technology in our own information age. Crystals are also powerful focusing tools that help people attain a deeper level of understanding. As such, they can assist you and your children in rituals that involve manifesting a goal, dealing with negative emotions, or healing. However, crystals are not magical; they are only tools. Although they have the power to help you, be careful that neither you nor your children invest in them any kind of mystic properties. In other words, don't give away your own power and expect crystals to do all the work.

CRYSTALS AND GEMSTONES

Amber: balance
Amethyst: spiritual awareness, transmutation, healing
Aquamarine: purification, healing, calming
Bloodstone: courage, physical energy
Calcite: balance, peaceful meditation
Carnelian: sex, self-esteem, creativity
Copper: purification, inspiring love, making peace
Fluorite: healing, releasing unwanted energies
Gold: courage, self-awareness, self-confidence, wealth, virtue
Hematite: encouraging willpower, concentration
Herkimer Diamond: dream recall
Jade: fertility, wisdom, tranquility, taking on the energy of the wearer
Lapis Lazuli: communication, healing
Malachite: protection, money
Moonstone: love, psychic awareness, feminine principle
Nickel: youth, beauty, growth, adaptation
Obsidian: inner growth, psychic development
Opal: passion, love, emotional expression
Pearl: purity, integrity, focus, wisdom

Quartz: change, focus
Red Jasper: compassion
Rhodolite: love
Rose Quartz: love, compassion
Silver: fertility, nourishment, growth
Tiger's Eye: empowerment, willpower, courage, clarity
Tin: flexibility
Topaz: new beginnings
Tourmaline: healing, balance
Turquoise: balance, connection with all life, friendship, positive thinking

Objects and Artifacts

Carl Jung theorized that symbols go directly into the brain, connecting you with the past. In almost every family ritual, you will use objects that carry certain meaning. Some will evoke what Joseph Campbell calls your own "personal mythology," stories that have been handed down from generations past, the sum of which add up to where you came from and who you are. In some rituals, you use traditional religious symbols, such as a statue of the Blessed Mother, pictures of angels, a Buddhist prayer wheel, or artifacts from other cultures, like a Native American talking stick (page 42). In child-focused rituals, you might include a security object, such as a blanket or stuffed animal, or a favorite toy; or you can use toy figures symbolically to represent members of the family. The objects employed in a ritual are limited only by your imagination. Below are everyday materials that are among the ingredients listed in many of the rituals I suggest, which can also be used to create objects of your own choosing.

✐ EVERYDAY MATERIALS YOU CAN USE ✐

Beads
Beans
Cardboard shoe boxes
Clay
Colored markers or crayons
Fabric and ribbon
Feathers
Flower pot
Glue
Gourds
Oatmeal cartons
Paint
Paper of assorted varieties
Pens and pencils
Personal treasures such as photos and
   jewelry
Rocks
Scissors
Seeds
Sewing needles and thread
Shells, rocks, leaves, or twigs
Silk flowers, pipe cleaners
Soil
Sticks (branches or chopsticks)
String or yarn
Tape

Animals

Many cultures have traditionally used animals as symbols. Native people often view animals as teachers, as each represents a beneficial quality that can help strengthen and educate a person. Families today are naturally drawn to the animal kingdom, too. Consider how important the family pet has become. Like the ancients, we also can learn from the animals. Just as we call on the strength of friends and family in time of need, in our rituals we can call on specific animals to support us. This is an easy concept for children to grasp, especially those who have a natural affinity toward animals. Once we understand each animal's essence—the specific gifts and strengths that creature represents—we can then incorporate a particular animal into a ritual and ask its guidance.

You might want to purchase a pack of Animal Medicine Cards at a bookstore or other type of store specializing in metaphysical tools, look for them on line, or send away for them. They are produced by Bear & Company in Santa Fe, New Mexico. The creators, Jamie Sams and David Carson, explain that native cultures have always connected animals to spirits, and they often look to animals as guides. When you're in a state of meditation, you pick one of the cards, and whatever animal comes up either guides you or teaches you something. Or, you can purposely choose an animal for its qualities. For instance, when little Jason was anxious about going into first grade, his mother gave him the lion card for courage. He carried it in his book bag for the first month of school.

If you don't have these cards, simply refer to the list below. Buy or, even better, make clay figurines or pictures to represent whatever animals you want to use.

❧ ANIMALS ❧

Bear: introspection, incubating ideas and bringing them to fruition, cultivating power and support

Beaver: architecture and building, teaches structure, problem solving, and the ability to work with others

Butterfly: transformation, moving forward, trusting life to support you

Cat: independence, playfulness, caution, gracefulness

Crow: intuition, justice

Deer: gentleness, peace

Dog: loyalty, guardian, protector

Dolphin: power of play, unconditional love, the ability to release stored emotions through breath

Dove: peace, calm, simplicity

Eagle: ability to see above the mundane, clarity, vision, connection to the divine

Fox: confidence, cunning, independence

Frog: connection to water rituals, a cleansing of spirit, body, and mind, easing change

Horse: power, dependability

Hummingbird: joy, celebration of life, the ability to feel emotionally "lighter"

Lion: leadership, action, assists one in moving through fear

Owl: wisdom, clairvoyance, clarity of thought

Peacock: wholeness, authority of self, the expression of one's own beauty

Rabbit: creativity, helps one face fear

Raccoon: unmasking the truth, helps one accept hidden aspects of the self, the ability to play many roles in life

Snake: sexuality, psychic energy, death and rebirth, immortality

Spider: integration, inner connection, creativity

Swan: ability to see one's own beauty and goodness

Tiger: confidence, spontaneity, strength

Turtle: connection with earth, grounding, helps one slow down and focus on the present

Wolf: teaching, the ability to set healthy boundaries, encourages friendship and sense of community

Physical Acts

In the rituals of many cultures, specific movements are performed to quiet the mind and imprint new behavioral patterns. Jews daven when they pray. Sufis whirl. Hindus and Buddhists assume certain yoga positions that affect the mind and body—for example, the Sun Salutation and *mudras,* which are sacred hand movements. These physical acts enhance your journey into a heightened state of awareness. For Hawaiian dancers, each hand gesture in the hula is sacred; in Bali, even the shifting of eyes is intrinsic to a dance ritual.

You don't need special training to experience the transformative power of physical acts. Singing, chanting, humming, dancing, and reciting poetry, as well as repetitive movements like pounding, drumming, rocking, swaying, or shaking a rattle can be incorporated into rituals you design. Activity is also wonderful in that it sustains the involvement of children who generally have a shorter attention span than adults. Even when a ritual doesn't call fo movement, you might want to include it when younger children are involved. Something as simple as walking in a circle can be a meditative act (see also walking meditation, page 26).

Of course, the key elements in any ritual are the people who participate in it. As I point out in the next chapter, you and your children have an abundance of "raw materials" in your hearts and minds, which can help you create meaningful traditions for your family.

3. The Raw Materials:

Making the Most of Your Heart, Mind, and Body

WITHIN EACH OF US lies an untapped source of peace, wisdom, and guidance. We often don't realize this, however, until we slow down, quiet our minds, tune into our bodies, and allow the creative juices to flow. The following basic techniques, to which I refer throughout the book, can help you do just that.

For children, the benefits are astounding. Learning to be conscious of their bodies and minds at a young age helps kids feel more in control of themselves and experience mastery over their environment. Children love to imitate their parents, so if they see you doing these techniques, they will emulate you. When kids start young, these practices become as natural to them as brushing their teeth. For example, Delia taught her daughter Amy deep breathing exercises at three. Today, at eight, whenever Amy has what she perceives as "a hard day" at school, she asks Delia, "Mom, will you help me do a relaxation?" And on a number of occasions, when her mother seems particularly stressed out, Amy has been known to suggest to Delia that *she* meditate!

Always do these exercises in a room that has a comfortable temperature and is free of distractions, such as a noisy clock or the recurrent hiss of a radiator. Turn off phones and answering machines, and remove pets from the room. For adults who have never done these techniques, I offer a basic approach that usually works with most older children, as well as ways to adapt the experience for younger ages. Bear in mind that there are developmental variations—some two-year-olds can sit still longer than some six-year-olds. Trust yourself; you know your own child and what he can handle, but also give him room to improve, which most kids do over time.

Conscious Breathing

Learning how to breathe is a prerequisite to ritual relaxation or any type of meditation or visualization. It is an important part of almost every ritual because it calms the participants and helps bring them into a sacred space.

Begin by explaining to your children that most of us never think about our breathing. We just do it. This exercise is to make us conscious, or aware, of that life-giving process. Sit quietly, make sure that your back is supported by a comfortable cushion, and close your eyes. Take a deep breath through your nose, inhaling as much air as possible into your body. Since this is probably the first conscious breath you've taken today, enjoy it. Allow the breath to move deep into your belly, filling it with air, expanding it. Some people call this a "belly breath." Then exhale slowly through your mouth. Continue breathing in through your nose to the count of four, hold for the count of two, and exhale slowly through your mouth to the count of four. Take slow deep breaths and focus only on your breathing—in and out, in and out, in and out. Repeat until you feel calm and relaxed.

The only difference in teaching deep breathing to very young children is that you might need to change some of the words you use to describe the process. Also, don't worry about whether the child is breathing in through his nose and out through his mouth; this will come naturally in time.

Have the child sit cross-legged on the floor or on a cushion, or even lie down if that's more comfortable. Begin by telling her to put her hands on her tummy and close her eyes. You might say, "Take a big, slow, deep breath. Pretend that you are a balloon and fill yourself with air. Feel it coming into your belly. Now gently blow the air out until it feels like there's nothing left in you." Repeat these instructions several times. Stress that she must do everything very slowly. "Do you feel how the air is filling you up and then leaving your body? This is called a belly breath." Have her continue practicing for one or two minutes at most.

When a child is tired, especially if he chooses to lie down, there's a good chance that a few minutes of deep breathing will put him to sleep, which is fine so long as no one criticizes him for it. Remember that the goal is for him to understand and feel the difference between everyday breathing and deep breathing. With children under six, it's probably a good idea to work one-on-one at first rather than in a group. Once the child learns how to breathe deeply, ideally in the sitting position, he can join older siblings.

With children over six, you can add counting to this exercise: "Breathe in, one, two. Breathe out, one, two." In time, the child will be able to increase the length of each breath (up to a four count as described above). Even with slightly older children, start only with a few minutes and gradually increase the time to ten or even twenty minutes.

Meditation

Meditation is a good way for members of your family to learn how to trust their intuition and innate wisdom. It goes a step further than simple deep breathing in that it sustains the process, not only relaxing the body but also quieting the mind. I begin each day by spending at least twenty minutes meditating. However, this isn't so easy with small children underfoot. Many parents I know attain a relaxed, meditative state in many other ways—walking, swimming, gardening, or simply lying on the ground and watching the clouds roll by. Some get the most out of absolute quiet, while others prefer music; some take this as private time, while others use these precious moments to connect with their children. In fact, whether done alone or with kids, these practices not only calm you, they put you into a *heart-centered* space. That is, instead of letting the often-critical and overanalytical mind lead the show, they allow your innate compassion and love to guide you and strengthen your family bonds.

If you've never meditated, though, be patient with yourself. It takes practice. Jack Kornfield, author of *A Path with Heart,* says that learning meditation is like training a puppy. You give the puppy a command—for example, "Stay"—and, despite many, many of your attempts, he's likely not to listen. In fact, as Kornfield points out, he's likely to make some kind of mess instead. "Our minds are much the same as the puppy," he writes, "only they create even bigger messes. In training the mind, or the puppy, we have to start over and over again."

To begin, sit in a cross-legged position with eyes closed. Take several deep belly breaths as described above. As an aid in relaxing your mind, you may also choose to repeat a mantra, a simple one-syllable word, like "peace" or "om," as you exhale each deep breath through your mouth. Allow the tone and your breath to become one. Try to focus on your heart for a minute or two, and you will see that the chaos in your mind quiets, and you will find a deeper relationship with your inner wisdom and capacity to heal. The most profound connections take place within the heart. If you or your children have never meditated, sit for only five minutes at first and, if you like, gradually increase the time.

Kids easily grasp simple meditation techniques. Several years ago, while working on *The Dr. Fad Show,* a television program for children, I taught the kids, who were between eight and thirteen, to do relaxation exercises before going on the air. We did elementary deep breathing, in which I instructed them to take long, slow, deep breaths, while imagining that their hands were getting warm. Focusing on a particular part of the body helps children feel more centered and in touch with themselves. The simple, quiet meditation calmed them down so that they could go on television without being nervous. I also know parents who have started their children meditating as young as three, or at least doing relaxation exercises.

The most important point to remember is to start small. The younger the child, the shorter the attention span. However, personality is also a factor. Some kids can better clear their minds by moving—say, swaying rhythmically or walking at a measured steady pace—while others are able to sit still for long periods without getting fidgety. In this respect, children are not much different from adults.

With children, of course, simple is often better. Here are two easy meditative exercises that work well with adults and that even young children can grasp:

℮ Walking meditations require the participants to slowly traverse a large circle or a predetermined path. In the last few years, in fact, many have made it a practice to "walk the labyrinth," a re-creation of the maze-like design originally found on the floor of Chartres and other magnificent cathedrals in Europe. Dating back to the Middle Ages and symbolizing the great pilgrimage to Jerusalem, the labyrinth, which has only one pathway leading into and back out of the center, represents the powerful inward journey in search of God and self.

Whether you walk the labyrinth, a wooded path, or the circumference of your living room, in this type of meditation the idea is to be conscious of your entire body and its movements while emptying your head of meaningless chatter. Thich Nhat Hanh, a Buddhist monk and author of *The Long Road Turns to Joy: A Guide to Walking Meditation,* suggests walking mindfully with a smile on your face. Notice each breath, he suggests, and practice counting the number of steps you take in as you breathe in and out.

℮ A grounding exercise, which can help you connect to the powerful resource of earth, is adapted from a Hawaiian standing meditation. It can be done indoors, but it is probably easier and more enjoyable for children to do outside. Try it whenever you or your child need support.

Start by taking several belly breaths. Close your eyes and imagine that you're a tree. From the bottom of your feet, picture your roots extending into the earth. Feel your roots connect with the earth and, in your mind's eye, see them going deeper and deeper. Let them go so deep that they touch the heart of Mother Earth. Take another deep breath and feel yourself drawing up energy from the earth. Let the energy move up into your roots and into your body. Feel how strong you are becoming. Let Mother Earth support you.

With any kind of meditative activity, experiment with your child, and never make it feel like a chore. It's better to stop any of these exercises than to risk your child's becoming upset and unwilling. Remember that children pick up whatever you're feeling; if you're aggravated or impatient or feel that they're not doing this "right," they know it and, chances are, they're not going to be eager to join you in the future. Kids also are more likely to be distracted when they are very hungry or immediately after eating, so time these exercises accordingly.

Visualization/Guided Imagery

The deepest part of your imagination is an untapped resource of wisdom and creativity. Learn to harness its power and teach your children to do it, too. In countless studies, scientists have proven that you can actually have a conversation with your body; in turn, it talks to your brain, which then directs your nervous system's response. *Calm down. Be confident. Be proud of yourself. Heal. Choose new solutions.* Visualization serves as a means to transmit these positive messages.

What, exactly, *is* visualization? I think of it as a self-told story that calms your body and sets your mind in a particular direction—a way of connecting your mind, body, and spirit. A visualization can relax or heal you, dredge up emotions that you need to release, ease anxiety, inspire creativity, and provide guidance. Like meditation, successful visualization allows your body to move into the so-called relaxation response—your heart slows, your mind clears, your muscles relax. Some people naturally do this better than others—psychologists refer to them as "high absorbers," people who direct their bodies with their minds more easily.

But remember that mastering visualization is a *process*; you and your children will get better with practice. In fact, children, because they have such free imaginations, are often better at this than their parents. When they close their eyes, they often see clear pictures in Technicolor. (By the way, it's okay if you never actually *see* pictures; chances are, you will find other ways to visualize—hearing sounds or feeling sensations.)

To do a visualization—or to help direct your children in one—you can either follow my script (see Box, page 29) or create one of your own, which can include some or all of the components listed below. Either way, you may want to make an audiotape of the instructions so that you can play them back and, as a family, peacefully experience their power. Guided imagery usually . . .

꙳ . . . sends your mind to a special space.

You can choose to be in a garden, at the beach, in the woods, a historical site you've been to or read about, a space capsule zooming through the heavens, or a fantasy spot, as long as it is *yours* and feels safe. With an adult or older child you would simply say, "Imagine a place that makes you feel safe and happy." But you might want to prompt a younger child: "Remember how great it felt when we were at the beach and the sun warmed your skin? Go back to that time and place." Encourage them to be inventive.

꙳ . . . engages all your senses.

You can also spur children's imaginations by asking questions. The more one's senses are engaged, the faster the body responds and the more effective the exercise will be. When you arrive at that special place, what do you see and hear? What scents and textures surround you? A high absorber might even be able to taste the experience.

꙳ . . . asks you to contact a "wisdom figure."

At the end of a long path, or behind a door that you open, there will be a family elder, a teacher, a spiritual leader, a mythological figure, a religious symbol, or simply colors and light that seem to lead to wisdom. This is what's called the wisdom figure. Some people don't necessarily see a person but they sense a presence. Be open to the endless possibilities. Your wisdom figure may be a surprise. And, particularly with children, he/she/it may change over time. Mine has always been an ageless woman with a loving and compassionate heart. My friend's nine-year-old son, Bailey, often sees a Power Ranger in his visualizations. Your children may see their favorite teachers or other superheroes whom they associate with power and wisdom.

꙳ . . . helps you ask for guidance.

Once you have connected with your own wisdom figure, ask any definitive questions that come to mind. *What should I do next? Why do I feel this way? What do I need to know right now? What will make me feel fulfilled?* You may have a specific question for a particular problem. Ask away. After you have practiced this exercise and feel confident in your wisdom figure's ability to answer, you can even ask "yes" or "no" questions, such as *Am I on the right track?* But in the beginning, it's best to be specific.

A Guided Meditation*

CLOSE YOUR EYES and take a few deep breaths. Allow your body to take in all of the air it needs. Slowly breathe in and out, in and out, in and out.

Now imagine yourself in a special place—a place that makes you feel happy and safe. It doesn't matter if it's a real place or one you imagine. Maybe it's a magical garden, a wonderful beach you once visited, a clearing in the woods, or a special room. It is beautiful and peaceful, and it's your private place where you can come to relax and receive guidance. No one can come here unless you invite them. This is your safe place.

Look around your special place. Imagine that you can touch something—a rock, a blade of grass, grains of sand, a soft blanket. In your imagination, feel the object. Now tune into the scents of this place—the perfume of the flowers, the salt of the sea, the fresh clean air of the forest. In your imagination, smell the aroma. Let yourself hear the sounds—birds singing, music playing, leaves rustling. In your imagination, listen to the sounds of this place. Pretend that you can ingest something in the room—a juicy apple, a crispy coconut, a succulent plum, a piece of chocolate. Taste one of these delicacies. Finally, pretend that you are the star of your own movie, and this is the set. Look around and observe the colors, the objects, the people, the animals. See your wonderful place. With all five senses at work, you feel calm and happy.

Now when I count to three, a special guide—a wisdom figure—will come to you. He or she may look like someone you know, or may be a spiritual figure, someone from history, or a TV character. Your guide may even be an animal, an angel, or a magical creature the likes of which you've never seen before. No matter what he, she, or it looks like, your guide is coming to your special place to give you advice. Your guide is your personal helper.

One . . . two . . . three . . .

Greet your guide and ask anything you want to know. Understand that your wisdom figure loves you and wants the best for you. Feel how happy and safe you feel in its presence. Take a moment to talk to her. Listen to what she has to say. Answers may come to you as a picture or in words.

Now it's time to say good-bye. Know that you can come here and be with your guide anytime you want. Take three deep breaths and then open your eyes. One . . . two . . . three . . . open your eyes.

---

*Recite the following instructions into a tape recorder. Pause fifteen to thirty seconds between paragraphs to allow time for your listeners to create their own images.

Creating an Altar

We tend to think of an altar as something found in a house of worship. That's true—but why can't you and your family also have one at home, or even more than one? It's one of the best ways I know to bring the sacred into your everyday life. Wherever an altar is placed—on a table in the family living room or kitchen, inside a desk at work or a locker at school—it will transport you away from everyday concerns and connect all of you to something larger than yourselves.

Altars, which are an integral part of many rituals, can be for an individual or for a group: A *personal* altar should reflect your aspirations, so make it uniquely yours. Think of it as a message board to the universe—a way of sending direct communications to God. For example, when eleven-year-old Ian seemed to be having trouble with schoolwork, his mother suggested that he create an altar to help build his confidence. On a blue cloth (for clarity), he placed a quartz crystal for focus and a gold star, which signifies self-confidence and achievement. Whenever he gets a good grade, he leaves the paper or test on the altar for a few days, as a reminder of his own excellence. Maria, a senior in high school, has an altar devoted to the college she'd like to attend. On it is a picture of the school and a mug she bought when she visited the school. Maria often takes time to sit at her altar, closing her eyes and imagining herself as a freshman on campus; she drops a penny into the mug for good luck.

I strongly recommend that couples and families create a *group* altar, with each person placing something on it that is special to them. In this way, the altar weaves together personalities and experiences to provide a sense of wholeness and connection. Newlyweds Peter and Jennifer placed pictures of their spiritual teacher and close friends on their altar, and they regularly light incense and candles to manifest their dreams. The Guerdons and their two children are saving money for a trip to Yosemite, and on their altar they have Davy's rabbit's foot and Tara's heart charms for good luck, as well as photos of the park. And in the Verona family, the parents, Kathy and Tony, keep a statue of the Virgin Mary at the center of the altar to represent their faith: Kathy donated a piece of her grandmother's jewelry to remind the family of its lineage; and Tony wrote positive affirmations ("We will take time for ourselves as a family") on the altar. Their ten-year-old, Patsy, made a drawing, sixteen-year-old Wesley wrote a poem, and even three-year-old Thomas added one of his tiny play figures. Whenever the Veronas take a vacation, the children always bring back offerings for the altar to remind them of that happy time.

With either individual or group altars, the symbols you choose to place on your altar will reinforce your intention. For example, in the

Family Reunion ritual (page 104), you will put pictures of your family and symbolic items that represent family memories on your altar; when mourning a dog's death (page 149), you will use objects that the animal wore or played with. Altars can be designed for specific purposes, too. I have three in my home: one in my bedroom dedicated to relationships, another in my office with items relating to success and prosperity, and a third in my living room, devoted to healing and meditation.

Your attention will be energized by the objects you choose to place on the altar, so select items that matter to you—make it personal and beautiful. For family altars, choose objects that are appropriate given the ages of your kids. And if you have very young children, consider safety factors—avoid toxic substances and keep dangerous items out of their reach.

Each time you glance at your altar, it will remind you of the things that are most important to you and of the support available to you. You can change it weekly, seasonally, or whenever you feel the need to bring in new energy or ideas. Sacred space that is used repeatedly over time builds emotional, energized charges. Even if you do none of the rituals I suggest, creating an altar will constantly remind you that a Divine presence works in your life. That is why even nomadic people keep altars.

Altars can be permanent, temporary, and/or portable. A *permanent altar* can be established on a chest, a small table, or on the floor. Find a spot that won't be disturbed, and make sure there's enough room around it, so that members of your family can sit or kneel together. Place a cloth over the area, then fill your altar with meaningful symbols: pictures of your loved ones, an object that connects you to nature (like a shell, a leaf, or a stone), a reminder of a teacher or wise, loving friend. If you want to strengthen your connection to Spirit, include a religious figure or symbol, and try to have something signifying each element—fire, water, air, earth.

A *temporary altar* is one that you create for a specific ritual. Set it up wherever you think it will have the greatest power—for example, create one in your child's room to celebrate the first day of school. Don't be afraid to be adventurous. Some of my favorite items come from toy stores and craft fairs. Use natural settings—arrange stones around a tree or seashells and seaweed at the shore.

A *portable altar* should fit into a small box or case that is easy to carry. It can include a candle, a symbol of Spirit, some incense, a vial of essential oils, a beautiful cloth. This is good to take on family trips or to give to a child going away to camp or school.

Some rituals don't require an altar in the strictest sense of the word and are more spontaneous and flexible. However, it is always a good idea to use an altar when you can to increase the ritual's power. Keep your altar as a place of reverence. Don't leave coffee mugs or yesterday's mail on it. Let it be an environment in which everyday moments can become precious jewels, manifesting as pure, invisible Spirit.

Getting Started

Once you've become familiar with the implements, ingredients, and raw materials in your pantry, you're ready to cook. The next three steps are preparation (put that apron on), process (get cooking), and follow-up (enjoy the finished product).

The first step involves *intention*. As I discussed in the Introduction (page xv), intention is one of the key elements of a ritual. A good way to plan rituals is to have a Family Meeting (pages 41–46). Take a few moments together and talk about why you and your family want to do this ritual. What do you all hope to gain from it? Remember that rituals should be done with an open heart, *never* to manipulate another human being. Write down everyone's ideas, ideally on a large pad that everyone can see. Try to imagine how the ritual will benefit you and your children. Be clear about your goals and careful in the planning. For example, choose a time to do the Family Meeting ritual (page 41) when no one is tired, hungry, or under pressure to get a project completed. Or, if two siblings have been at each other all day, although you'd like them to do a ritual for Healing a Rift (page 137), ask yourself if *they* are really ready to give up the battle. If they're not ready to talk out the problem, even in safe ritual space, it might be best to hold off. Take into consideration the youngest child's level of understanding and try to keep the discussion on a level that he or she can grasp. It's hard for a child to focus on a ritual if he or she doesn't understand what's going on. If you are using a recipe from this book, familiarize yourself with it first, and then explain to the others exactly what it involves, so that everyone can participate at the deepest level.

Next, *assemble your ingredients*. I've given you an entire supermarket full of ingredients that you might include, but don't get caught up in having it be perfect. If you can't find an object, have everyone pitch in and make it. Even young children can cut pictures out of magazines; older kids can draw or sculpt objects out of clay. Mom or Dad could carve an artifact out of wood. If the recipe calls for a yellow candle and you can't find one, use white, the universal color. Have the kids make candles themselves or decorate a white one with food coloring or colored stones.

Where will you conduct your ritual? Location can affect the quality of your experience. Whether it's a backyard, living room, bedroom, or basement, the area should be free from distractions and interruptions. If you're inside, turn off the phone and fax machine, and hang a "Do Not Disturb" sign on your door.

Remember that a ritual must have a sacred space (page 3). The simple act of lighting a candle, burning incense, ringing a bell, or sprinkling salt or water can sanctify a space. Some people remove their shoes when entering a ritual space or wash their hands with scented water to symbolize leaving the outside world for a brief moment in time. I always have a bowl of sage water near my front door for my friends to wash their hands (use plain water for young children). This eases the transition from the outside noise of New York City to a quiet and calm atmosphere.

You also need to have a clear sense of *beginning and ending* (page 3). You can turn music on, light a candle, take a deep breath, or just say, "I am now beginning." Close your eyes and find your heart center as you embark on your journey. For a formal ending, blow out the candle, say "thank you" or "Amen," or have a quiet moment of reflection, followed by a final deep breath.

In many rituals, I include a *follow-up* suggestion. Remember that rituals are symbolic rites that unlock doors to a new awareness, healing, and state of being. But a ritual is only the key that opens the door. Once you walk through, you must find ways to continue the process and to create new patterns for success. Children, especially, learn best from repetition, and because rituals bring an element of predictability into their lives, they love to do them over and over. Follow-up suggestions vary. For example, if you have an annual family reunion, I might suggest that you plan another event within the next few months. However, some rituals, such as seasonal celebrations, require only a yearly update; and others, which commemorate a one-time event, like a youngster's starting a new school, do not necessarily require any follow-up.

What Children Can Handle

Children love to help out in the kitchen—the *ritual* kitchen as well. This entire book is about sharing rites and ceremonies with the family, so ask your children to contribute their ideas. Kids have a natural inclination toward ritual; their imagination lends creativity and inspiration that will delight and amaze you. In these pages, I have included some powerful rituals that young children have created to help themselves deal with life's sorrows and joys. However, you must always ask yourself what is developmentally appropriate for *your* children. Keep in mind the length of the ritual, a child's attention span, and the nature of the recipe. The younger your children, the shorter the ceremony should be. Use the following chart as a guideline, but also trust your instincts. Always avoid practices that seem dangerous to conduct or are too long or too complicated for your children to follow. And never force kids to do rituals. Make them inviting so that they will want to do them.

When planning rituals and pondering what your child can handle, allow for individual differences. Some three- to five-year-olds can sit no more than thirty seconds, whereas others, entranced in a story or art project, can sit for much longer. Trust yourself; you probably know what your child is capable of. If not, start small and build tolerance. Another good way to gauge your child's receptivity, readiness, and patience is to look at yourself: What do you like doing, what are your skills, and how long do you feel comfortable doing a ritual? Children often mirror our own endurance, so pay attention to how long it takes for you to get fidgety. It's a sure sign that your kid will get bored by then, too.

Rituals and Your Child: What's Appropriate?

	WHAT THEY LIKE	WHAT THEY CAN HANDLE	BE CAREFUL...
Under Three	Want to see and touch everything; love music, noise-making, and activity.	Attention span is very variable; plan rituals that don't require sitting still for long.	Keep these kids away from open flames, smoldering incense, or charcoal; beware of accidental ingestion of substances; anything too abstract will be lost on a toddler.
Three to Five	The "magic years" when they're beginning to use their imaginations; they have highly active fantasy lives, but rituals need to be fairly concrete for them to "get" the meaning.	Saying grace, lighting candles (with supervision); these kids can draw, paint, make puppets, use blunt scissors; they understand colors and may already have "favorites."	Children this age get scared easily; be careful that ritual doesn't trigger a child's fears; you can also plan a ritual to help a child deal with fears.
Six to Nine	This is when kids first begin to take tentative steps to separate from Mom and Dad, moving out of the family into the world; they like to plan and create; they're interested in learning about other cultures; love to help others; can stand a little delayed gratification.	Longer rituals are possible; these kids also like more elaborate arts and crafts projects, creating objects that require more than one sitting to complete; may play instruments; can write simple poems and prayers.	Structure is very important to these kids, so disruption of a regular routine or doing a ritual differently from the way you've done it before is likely to raise protest; these kids are obsessed with "rules."

(Continued on next page)

Rituals and Your Child (Continued)

	WHAT THEY LIKE	WHAT THEY CAN HANDLE	BE CAREFUL...
Ten and Older	Beginning to shape own beliefs and to understand issues of moral concern—what's "right" and what we can do to make ourselves or others feel better; may want to take a greater role in ritual planning and may even criticize *your* ideas; peers are also important to these kids, so you might want to include friends in rituals.	Developmentally, they can do pretty much what adult participants can do; can come up with very original ideas for rituals; able to work with symbols and less concrete ideas, but they don't fully grasp abstractions until their teen years.	If you're just starting to introduce rituals at this age, you might find some resistance; preteens and teens are deathly afraid of being "different" from their friends; they also might feel embarrassed by rituals, or think of them as being contrived or even "nerdy."

A Few Final Points to Remember

Here are a few final bits of advice before you set off on your ritual journey:

Keep It Simple. When you begin to create rituals, make them simple and clear. You can get more intricate as you gain confidence.

Never Let Material Constraints Detract from Creating Meaningful Experiences. If you don't have the exact object specified in a recipe or the perfect space to perform the ritual, work with what you do have. Improvise and be creative. There's no such thing as doing it wrong.

36

Don't Be a Slave to Directions. Veer from the recipes I suggest if they don't feel right for your family's style or personality. Sometimes, I'll suggest that a parent or a grandparent lead the ritual, but a teenager can do so as well. These rituals are suitable for all kinds of families, but if your family configuration seems to be different from what a description implies, adapt accordingly.

Be Open to New Possibilities. Think of creating rituals as making soup. I give you the basics, but it is up to you to season it to your own taste. Never do anything that contradicts your own belief system, but, at the same time, be open-minded. As you participate in rituals, you will notice that the universe lends its support so that miracles can occur. You will gain new insight into your life, greater connections will be forged between family members, new experiences will be easier to handle, rough times will be made smoother. Think of yourself as helping your family tune into the universal life force. See these experiences as part of a great adventure—follow a new route home, taste a new food, try something you've never done before. Look at your family and your lives with fresh eyes and discover hidden treasures. Imagine yourselves as tourists visiting a foreign country. Let your children guide you and allow your own inner child to come forth.

4. Everyday Rituals

LONG BEFORE there were computers, video games, and television sets in every room of the house, before themed family restaurants and amusement parks, families spent time together eating, playing, and sharing long evenings of reading and storytelling. Today, a number of studies reveal that while we all may live under the same roof, we're often in different rooms from our children, involved with our own activities and projects. Parents and children spend their days at work and school during the week, and on the weekends are usually involved in their own pursuits—Mom doing repairs around the house, Dad off playing golf, the kids lobbying to have friends over, see the latest "in" movie, or scurry off to the mall.

Meanwhile, a whole industry has been spawned by this phenomenon, including family restaurants where kids have their own activities, and centers, like Kidsport and Gymboree, solely devoted to children's amusement. Given their own busy schedules, parents often feel guilty about spending time away from their kids, and these child-centered activities seem to fill a void, says family therapist Ron Taffel. Still, they keep parents and children in different worlds.

But even in the daily frenzy of our chaotic lives, there are simple ways to reunite as a family, to connect with our children on a daily basis, and to give greater meaning to those moments of togetherness. Creating "everyday rituals" can turn ordinary moments into something precious and special. You can make home a safe refuge from the fast pace of modern life. No matter how chaotic your daily existence, rituals—however small and seemingly mundane—can center you and your family—and, in the process, create a foundation for new growth, celebration, and healing.

You can easily incorporate the following everyday rituals into your ordinary routines, such as meals, baths, and bedtime. Perhaps you already have your own variations on these themes, such as a nightly tuck-in and snuggle. I hope that the suggestions in this chapter help you become more conscious of the rituals that you're already doing, such as greeting the kids with milk and cookies after school, establishing a quiet hour for homework, or having a certain routine for after-dinner cleanup. Do what's comfortable and, if you like, include aspects of my rituals that appeal to you. All you need to do is add your own intention: fostering togetherness, cooperation, and connection.

~ *Family Meetings*

IN THE RUSH of your everyday life, do you find yourself making endless lists and appointments, developing systems to remember your briefcase and your kids' lunches? And even though you're organized and you know everyone's schedule, do you ever go to bed feeling that you haven't really talked to your children (or your spouse)? Do days or even weeks go by when family members don't say what's on their minds until someone finally explodes in anger or begins pouting in the privacy of his or her room?

If so, you have a typical family. Such dilemmas face many parents today, even those who have become adept "jugglers." That's why so many mental health practitioners recommend setting aside a specific time to be together as a family, to talk, and to listen to one another. This idea of "family meetings," first proposed by psychiatrist Rudolf Dreikurs in his 1964 book *Children the Challenge,* is an idea whose time has come. Many of us need to schedule meetings with our families the way we schedule work-related tasks or doctors' appointments.

I have adapted my Family Meeting ritual from the Hawaiian practice of *ho'opono pono,* which means "making right." Shown to me by my good friends Alan and Antoinette Alapi, it is used in healing and also in completing the day. Like many cultures living close to nature, the Hawaiians believe that since we are all connected, any individual problem, be it physical, emotional, or spiritual, is the result of an imbalance within the family. The ailing person is simply a manifestation of a problem in the larger community—the family or the village. Family therapists, who treat individuals as part of a larger system, operate on the same assumption. Sharing feelings regularly, they believe, helps maintain unity and balance because negativity never has a chance to build up and infect the group.

At a time when there has been so much focus

on blaming the family, *ho'opono pono* is a welcome relief. I have incorporated elements of it here to create a ritual that begins with the honest expression of feelings (good and bad) and emphasizes the spirit of forgiveness. In fact, this is the first ritual in the book because I see it as one which can be used not only to connect with one another but also with God, your Higher Power, or however your family defines Spirit. And, if you wish, it can also be a time when you plan and prepare for other rituals, or deal with other family concerns.

Intention: To bring the family into harmonious balance and then conduct whatever family business, practical or emotional, is necessary.
Timing: Ideally, once a week on a day and time specifically set aside for this purpose.
Ingredients: Matches, blue candle (communication), green candle (healing), essence of basil (mental clarity), talking stick (see below), bread, optional food and drink.

Making a Talking Stick: Many native cultures employ talking sticks in rituals, the idea being that whoever is holding the stick has the right to speak. No one is allowed to interrupt or criticize the talker. A simple twig or even a ruler can be designated as the family's talking stick, but it's also fun for everyone to get involved in creating one. Hunt for a good stick outdoors, at least one or two inches in diameter and two to three feet long—big enough to feel substantial, small enough for the youngest child to hold comfortably. If you're a city dweller, you can also saw off a portion of a mop or broom handle, or buy a rounded dowel at a hardware store. Your talking stick can be painted or colored with indelible markers. It can be decorated with everyone's name or initials; pictures or symbols; beads, stones, ribbons, or other decorative items. The important thing is that everyone has a hand in its creation.

The Planning Session: Before you do this ritual for the first time, it's a good idea to have a planning session, both to explain its purpose and to make a talking stick (see above). Tell the children that this will be a time for adults and children to say whatever is on their minds—anything that upset them, that made them feel good, or that they'd simply like to get off their chests. Stress that no one will be criticized or punished for any wrongdoing and that this is not a time to "get" someone else. When you share emotions, hurt and angry feelings may emerge, but by doing this ritual, you create a safe, sacred place, the intention being to heal and forgive.

Explain that having each person talk about his or her feelings, and then taking responsibility and acknowledging how that one person's actions affect the whole group, helps restore harmony to the family. Also, when we release feelings of anger and hurt, it brings our individual minds and bodies into balance as well.

Once you have become familiar with the recipe, you can expand the format to suit different purposes. However, the first part of the ritual—prayer, sharing, and forgiveness—should always be included. At the end, you can add a scheduling session (for chores and for fun) and/or conduct a group activity, such as making a dream pillow (page 58).

Recipe: Always begin by sitting in a circle to symbolize an unbroken connection. Light the two candles and say a prayer to bring in guidance. Use your own words or say something simple like, "Let us join together in love, to heal ourselves and share from our hearts." Put the essence of basil into a diffuser or a dish of warm water and explain that the aroma will help each person think more clearly.

Have each family member take a turn with the talking stick. You could start with the youngest person, ask a different person to go first every week, or simply go clockwise around the circle. The important thing is that everyone has a turn, sharing his feelings and reporting on the events of the week—from a fight at school to a promotion at work. If your daughter has been helped by another family member, she should express gratitude. If your son is carrying a grudge, feels hurt by another family member, or is frightened about something, this is a time when he can feel comfortable talking about it.

Although this is a ritual for sharing all feelings—positive or negative—in cases when a talker admits to a transgression against the group or a particular family member, he or she should also ask forgiveness and offer some form of restitution. You may have to help younger children think of ways they can pay their debts. Stress that this is not meant as punishment. All of us must be accountable for our actions. When children learn that there are consequences for their behavior, they become not only more responsible citizens, they feel better about themselves. For example, if a child admits he hasn't been doing his chores, he might offer to be better about handling his responsibilities in the future, and he might also ask if there's anything extra he can do around the house. Or, a child who has broken a toy or ripped a page out of a sibling's book might offer to give something of her own, or do chores to earn money to buy a new toy or book. (Parents should never use information that comes up in a family meeting to heap on extra chores, ground a child, or in other ways take away privileges, unless *the child himself* suggests it.)

Those who have been hurt then offer the child forgiveness. Sometimes, it's necessary for the parent to either set an example ("Thank you, Peter, for being so honest about this. I know it was hard for you to admit that you lied, but I forgive you") or step in and help open the hearts of family members who aren't so eager to forgive ("Lisa, I know you're angry at Bobby for breaking your toy, and I don't blame you. But Bobby is being honest, and he's offering to make up for what he did. Can't you find it in your heart to forgive him?").

Once everyone has had her turn, use your own words or offer this healing prayer: "God, we thank you for letting us share from our hearts and for helping us restore harmony to our family circle." Now pass a loaf of bread, a symbol of nourishment, around the circle, and invite each person to take a piece. This act implies that the family will never want for sustenance, and that its members will always nurture one another.

At this point, you can end the ritual by sharing favorite food and drink, playing music or singing songs, or even telling jokes. Or, you can then begin to discuss other family business, do a joint project of some type, or plan another kind of family ritual.

Follow-Up: Follow-up will depend on what happened in the family meeting. If you brainstormed ideas or planned to start a family project or make a trip, make sure there is follow-through on everyone's part. If a family member has expressed gratitude or any other positive feelings, the person or people on the receiving end might want to take notice of nice things that person does for them, with an eye toward mentioning them in the next family meeting. If someone has agreed to make amends, he or she must let the others know that the wrong has been set right or that restitution has been made. Initially, parents may have to prod children a bit, but in time the internal reward of taking responsibility for oneself is usually enough to encourage most kids to cooperate. Of course, if a parent is the one who committed the wrongdoing, the best form of teaching is to set a good example.

RITUAL REALITIES: More and more families nowadays are embracing the idea of family meetings. I'm sure there are as many variations on the theme as there are families. Here are two examples:

∼ Alan and Antoinette Alapi, who live in Hawaii, do the *ho'opono pono* ritual every night with their children, Amber, Ashley, Akane, and Alii. If the kids have sleep-over guests, their friends are included, too. They begin with a prayer for Spirit to guide them and then each has a chance to talk about his or her day. They end by playing the ukelele and singing songs.

∼ Because of their son's problems in school, the Delanos now have a family meeting once a week. Jean is a secretary, and her husband, Mike, works for the sanitation department. Jean had stopped working when their son, Mark, was born and continued to be an at-home mom until their second child, Terence, was in first grade. When she returned to work, life seemed to fly out of control. Between keeping the household running and chauffeuring one boy or the other to appointments, games, and friends' houses, Jean always felt frazzled. Mike worked long hours, and though he was committed to being a hands-on father, his time with the boys was limited. There was no such thing as a schedule in this family, much less time just to be together in a quiet and centered space. When Mark began having trouble in school, it was the final straw. As Jean sees it now, though, his difficulties were a blessing for the whole family.

The school psychologist diagnosed Mark as having attention deficit disorder and stressed that as long as Jean and Mike made sure there were predictable routines in the house and clear consequences for Mark's behavior, their son would do fine. And it wouldn't hurt Terence either. The psychologist also suggested family meetings. When Jean, who worked for a learning center I was associated with, told me what was happening in her family, I suggested that she think of a family meeting in its broadest sense, not just to help coordinate family life but to help foster connections. These meetings should give everyone a time to feel heard *and* held by the group.

Months later, when I ran into Jean at the center, she looked a lot happier. "I can't believe what a difference these family meetings have made," she offered. "Just knowing that every Sunday at five we all come together for quiet caring and listening has made us grow closer. Mark still gets out of control sometimes, but I can always say, 'This is something you should bring up at the family meeting.' And although he and Terence still squabble, like most brothers do, I've heard one say to the other, 'I'm bringing this up at the meeting.' It's much nicer than hearing, 'I'm gonna tell!'"

Mealtime Blessings

VIRTUALLY EVERY ARTICLE or book about healthy families encourages parents to eat with their kids. The truth is, most parents today recognize the importance of eating meals together as a family. We all know that sharing food is the ultimate symbol of nurturing and togetherness. But our lives are so busy that we often find ourselves eating on the run (don't tell me you've never grabbed a quick bite while driving or even standing up!) or wolfing down meals without paying much attention to what we're ingesting.

When it comes to our kids, we certainly *try* to eat together. In fact, 70 percent of the 2,500 parents and children polled in a 1990 study indicated that they had family dinners at least five nights a week. Not surprisingly, though, the frequency declines as children get older—their social lives become increasingly independent of their parents. Indeed, most parents report that often mealtimes are hectic, emotionally charged affairs. So while we're sitting at the same table, we're not on the same page!

We can make our meals together more civilized and sacred by honoring our food and becoming more conscious of what we're eating. I can't guarantee that siblings won't fight or little kids won't get fidgety, but if you start mealtime rituals when children are young, they learn to be grateful for their bounty. They also develop respect for food and a healthy consciousness of what it means to literally feed themselves. I suggest two mealtime rituals here: a simple one for everyday meals and a more elaborate one for a weekly family dinner.

Everyday Meals

People of virtually every religion say prayers and blessings over food, taking time to honor its sacredness. In Bali, for example, no family would sit down to eat without first offering small pieces

47

of sustenance and beauty to the spirits—*banten jutan* (banana leaf with rice and salt) and *canang* (palm leaves woven into little baskets into which flowers are placed). They then eat their food, sharing it as if they were having a communal meal with their ancestors and deities.

I have been heartened to see a similar trend taking hold in this country. Today, 63 percent of our population gives thanks before meals, compared to 43 percent in 1947. I've also started seeing families join hands in restaurants. Some cultures even eat in silence, the idea being that you never take food for granted. You become more aware of what you eat, you are mindful of the act of eating, and you set a clear intention: to be nourished. By blessing our food, we literally encourage the nutrients to interact with our bodies and sustain us.

Intention: To appreciate and give thanks for the nourishment in our lives and to create an atmosphere of mindful eating.
Timing: Before every meal.
Ingredients: Make the table beautiful by using flowers, candles, and homemade decorations. Use fruit and food as symbols of nurture, love, attention, and care. You might also have a special item—a goblet, a plate, or candle sticks—that is used only when you all eat together.

Creating "Grace": Grace is a simple prayer or silent moment that acknowledges the blessings we have been given. If your family already says grace before meals, then say it before this ritual. If not, before you do this ritual for the first time, come up with a mealtime blessing (perhaps at one of your Family Meetings; see page 41). It can be a religious prayer, a poem that you find in the library, something the family writes together, or you can use or adapt the one I have suggested below. It can be the same for every meal, or you can have everyone take turns, reading blessings or poems they have composed for this sacred purpose.

Grace

May this food that we are about to eat

Give us health and nourishment.

We give thanks for all our blessings.

We give thanks to Life.

Recipe: Begin by holding hands. Have everyone close their eyes and take a deep breath. Allow each family member and/or guest to have a turn at reciting a prayer of thanksgiving. Depending on what meal this is, you might also wish to say a sentence or two about your plans. Breakfast, for example, is also a good time to set your intention for the day ("As we go into the day, may we be blessed with energy and creativity"). At dinner, you might offer thanks for getting over a cold, for having a great day at work or school, or for winning the softball game. Or, you might thank the stove for cooking the food, the garden for giving you vegetables, the baker for the fresh bread. Children love to do this—it's like a game but, at the same time, one that makes them conscious of the good in their lives.

Weekly Family Dinner

So many of us remember with fondness the days when the extended family dropped by for Sunday dinner, and Mom put out a spread of our favorite foods. Later, the relatives, arriving with armfuls of ethnic favorites, added their offerings to the table. Typically, after Sabbath services, families have a special meal—Italians dine together after church, Jewish people have Friday night suppers, and for generations African Americans have come home from "meeting Sundays" to have a huge family dinner together (a tradition beautifully portrayed in the film *Soul Food*).

Clearly, these communal eating traditions nourish more than our bodies. "The most important thing about a meal isn't the food," stresses Ruth Reichl, former food critic for the *New York Times*. "It's that we sit down together, we stop and pay attention to each other, and we talk."

Timing: Once a week set a definite day to which all members commit.
Ingredients: Festive table decorations (homemade artifacts, leaves, or flowers), favorite foods, matches, a candle for each member of family, rosemary (bonding).

Recipe: Set a specific time for dinner. In this ritual, the idea is to prepare an offering for your family. Therefore, the preparation itself is as important as actually eating the meal. Every member of the family, even small children with Mom or Dad's help, should be allowed a turn at being in charge—deciding what to serve, decorating the table, and assigning jobs to everyone in the family to make it happen.

The planner might want to use themed decorations that relate to a time of year, special interests, a holiday, or to honor a person. For example, Mom may choose a flower theme to show off the spring flowers she grew. Dad could take out old photos of his father and mother, who died before the children were born, and use this opportunity to help the children understand more about his own childhood and parents. A teenager might create a football-inspired table and share a story about his escapades on the junior high team. A young child might create a table with items related to her favorite new doll.

The meal itself can be very simple—peanut butter and jelly sandwiches if your five-year-old is in charge, pancakes when it's Dad's turn, pizza when a teenager is at the helm. When a person chooses a food, she gives a gift of herself and makes a commitment to the family unit. As Reichl points out, "When a mother cooks a meal, or a father, or whoever, you're giving your family something of yourself."

The important thing is that you all share your favorite foods and are open to trying new things, even to creating recipes of your own. If you have a garden, you also might want to make use of fresh ingredients that connect your family to a communal source of nourishment—the earth. If a very young child wants the meal to include foods that are too difficult for him to make, he can assign jobs to his older siblings and parents.

If you invite your extended family or friends, involve them in the preparation as well. Remember that with all of this—the decoration, the preparation, the food—it's the intention that counts. Doing work in the kitchen develops skills and teaches responsibility to children, but more important, these times will create positive memories for everyone.

When the table is set, and all the food has been prepared, you're almost ready to enjoy the meal. First, light the candles, dedicating each one to a family member. Each time you light a candle say, "I send my love to [name of family member]." Hold up the rosemary and say, "Let this represent our connection and our wish that every day we will grow stronger together as a family." Now hold hands, close your eyes, and take a deep, cleansing breath. The person in charge of the meal should say grace, either the prayer used for your family's everyday meals, or one that he or she has prepared for this particular meal.

Follow-Up: Keep a calendar in clear view with the person's name on the date that he or she is in charge.

RITUAL REALITY: Thirty-five-year-old Gina, a super-organized single mother of two, lives on a very tight schedule. Her alarm goes off at six, when she catches up on her reading and does her morning exercises. Her kids, Bill and Annie, ages five and eight, get up at seven o'clock and know the routine: wash, dress, get book bags together, and set the table for breakfast—which always includes a silk rose in a vase, to bring in love and joy. This family would never start the meal without saying grace. "They know it's important for us to eat together and to give thanks for all we have. It also calms them before school," says Gina.

Interestingly, Gina didn't grow up in a family that had much respect for rituals. Dad was a traveling salesman, and Mom often had her meals standing in the kitchen, while Gina and her brother ate in front of the TV. No one ever said grace before meals. Holidays were a slap-dash affair. "I was always amazed when I went to kids' houses where everyone sat together at dinner. Unlike my family, there was a sense that you could depend on certain things happening. I knew I wanted that in my life, too."

And Gina has done just that. Every day there's a predictable routine in her family. After she drops off the children at the local elementary school, she commutes to her own job as the director of a charitable foundation. Her ex-husband, an artist who works out of his home, picks the children up after school, and they play at his house until Gina comes at five-thirty. Their evenings are similarly regimented, with specific times for homework, dinner, a game, bath, bedtime cuddles.

But the high point of everyone's day is the family's daily candlelit dinner. "It makes us all feel more civilized." Again, no one touches his or her food until a simple prayer is offered in thanks: "God, we thank you for all that you provide."

Every Sunday, Gina has a dinner that includes not only blood relatives but her extended family of friends and their children. Since her divorce, she and her children look forward to these weekly dinners because they affirm the love and support that surrounds them. Instead of taking on the entire expense and the burden of preparation, however, it's pot luck; everyone, no matter how young or old, is asked to contribute a favorite food. Sometimes, especially on holidays, they have theme dinners or a meal features particular ethnic foods. Gina says her favorite dinner was one where everyone was asked to bring "comfort foods," and they feasted on such all-time favorites as spaghetti and meatballs, chicken soup, and S'mores.

~ Bathing

FROM THE BEGINNING of history, baths have been used to purify the spirit, cleanse the body, and uplift the soul. Many cultures use water in purification rituals. In the Greek Orthodox tradition, holy water is sprinkled over the altar. After a funeral, the Maori Indians in New Zealand chant at the deceased person's home and sprinkle water in every corner. And in a Shinto temple in Japan, one must wash both hands and mouth before entering.

Baths have also been used for beautification and pleasure. Cleopatra took baths in milk and honey to soften her skin. The early Roman baths contained theaters and libraries in which philosophers and writers lounged on intricately carved marble seats and discussed their latest works. And the *Kama Sutra,* the fourth-century Sanskrit treatise on erotica, instructs lovers in the sensual art of bathing. Even today, the communal baths in Japan are not for physical cleansing; they are a social event, a time for families (and even friends) to come together. Contrary to how we Westerners view bathing, the Japanese wash themselves with soap and a brush before stepping into the communal bath. Afterward, the family has tea and other refreshments.

Unfortunately, in our own modern obsession with health and cleanliness, we have lost some of the deeper, more spiritual connections to bathing. Why shouldn't children and adults in America use bathing as a transition between the business of the day and the quiet of the evening? Again, this is an activity we already do. And by simply acknowledging our intention, an ordinary bath becomes transcendent, enabling the bather to shed stress and apprehension. I strongly recommend including a bath as a part of the evening ritual, because it has such a quieting effect and because there's usually more time before bed. However, depending on what's most convenient and appropriate for your family, you also can include bathing in your morning routine.

Following are two suggestions, one tailored to a child who cannot take a bath unattended, the other for adults and older children. In both cases, the intention and timing are the same.

For Children Who Cannot Be Left Unattended

Intention: In the morning, to prepare mentally for the day ahead; in the evening, to unwind and relax after a stressful day.
Timing: At least once or twice a week.
Ingredients: Bathtub, warm water, hypoallergenic color tablets, fresh flowers, oatmeal and muslin bath bag (see below), gentle children's bubble bath or shampoo, towel, squeeze bottle, and essential oils, chosen according to personal appeal and purpose and/or changed seasonally or for special occasions. For example, in a nighttime ritual, use calming scents and teas like chamomile or lavender; for morning, use geranium (relieves anxiety) and lemon or orange (energy). *Optional:* Add a drop of rose oil for dry skin or vanilla to bring a joyous feeling into the room.

To Make a Bath Bag: Place rolled oats (store-bought oatmeal will do) in a muslin bag or cotton cloth, and tie it closed with string, or tie the fabric in a knot. When it's held under running water, the oats soften, and as the tub fills, the water turns milky. Kids love the slimy texture and it's good for their skin.

Recipe: To make a child's bath time magical, allow at least twenty minutes, without outside interference or interruption. Use some or all of the ingredients suggested above. Make the water your child's favorite color by using the hypoallergenic tablets. Let her pretend to be swimming in juice or an imaginary sea. Shower her with flowers as you place a make-believe crown on her head, dubbing her queen for the evening. She will love washing with the muslin bag. Use the squeeze bottle to rinse the shampoo out of her hair. If you use essential oils, place only one or two drops into the water. This is not recommended for infants; and even with children from age one to three, use only one drop.

If this is a nighttime bath, make it your child's time to relax and prepare for a restful sleep. If a morning bath, make it a time for the child to feel energized and purified and ready for the day ahead. Either time, gently encourage her to share news and, especially, to talk about anything upsetting. Explain that by talking about these things in the tub, she can wash away any fears or cares. Then, when you lift her or she steps out of the bath, snuggle her into a special towel and allow her to watch her worries go down the drain.

RITUAL REALITY: Marla, a
television producer, came to me because her five-year-old son Brendan, who had recently entered kindergarten in a new school, was having trouble falling asleep at night. I asked her about their evening rituals, and she told me she always read him a story and tucked him into bed. Brendan took baths in the morning with his dad, so that wasn't part of his normal nightly routine. I suggested that for a few weeks she try something different, not only giving Brendan a bath in the evening but also making it a special, calming ritual. Marla was reluctant to interrupt Brendan's routine, especially because he so looked forward to the morning shower with his father. "Why not bathe him twice?" I asked, pointing out that his evening baths could be more like a Japanese ritual—for calming, rather than cleansing.

That night, Marla told Brendan she would prepare a special bath for him that would help him feel "soft inside and good all over" but she needed his help. Marla already had a supply of essential oils at home that she used in her own rituals, so she let Brendan sniff them and decide which was his favorite. She had just bought a new loofah sponge for herself, but she decided to give it to Brendan. "I told him it was just for

him, and that using it would make his body tingle. When Brendan was in the tub, Marla spoke to him quietly and asked him to concentrate on feeling how good the warm water felt. She had him start using the loofah on his toes and work his way up until he had rubbed every part of his body. Then she scrubbed his back. She told him, "All of your fears are in the water now, Brendan. We've rubbed them all off." She instructed him to get out of the tub and watch them all go down the drain with the water. "You should have seen the look in his eyes," she recalls. "He looked really happy and calm."

Even at five, Brendan was old enough to appreciate the effects of his nightly baths. Marla kept up the two-baths-a-day routine until Brendan was comfortable in school. Most of the time, he still showers with his dad in the morning, but every now and then he asks, "Mom, can you give me a special bath tonight?"

For Older Children and Adults

Ingredients: Bathtub, warm water, sea salt (purification), essential oils chosen for their appeal and/or meaning—a combination of scents such as neroli (joy, purification), lemon (health), geranium (happiness), lavender (soothing), or ylang-ylang (peace, love), matches, purple candle (release), towels, herb tea or honey water.

Optional: Lavender oil and additional candles for mood lighting.

Recipe: Place a "Do Not Disturb" sign on the door and ask family members to honor it. If you have a large family, you might have to negotiate in advance how much time you have—ideally, at least twenty minutes. As you run the warm water and watch it fill the tub, set your intention, depending on whether it's a morning or evening bath. Into the tub, pour the sea salt and a total of six to seven drops of whatever combination of essential oils you have chosen. Light the purple candle to symbolize the release of all your negative emotions—if in the morning, your anxieties about what lies ahead; if at night, your cares from the day. (You may want to turn off the lights and light additional scented or nonscented candles to turn the bathroom into a meditation room.)

Before you step into the bath, remove your daytime clothes consciously and slowly, symbolically letting go of the mundane and ordinary. Once in the tub, lie back and soak. This will release all the stress and tension from your body and alleviate your concerns about the day. Feel the sea salt draw the impurities from your body. Breathe deeply and allow the essential oils to permeate your being. If you have headache tension, also rub a little lavender oil over your temples.

With each exhalation, concentrate on releasing negativity and fear. Allow all your worrisome thoughts to dissolve in the water. Take as much time as you need to replenish your mind, body, and spirit.

Always have clean towels (even better, warm ones, straight from the dryer) to wrap yourself in after the bath. Sip some warm tea or honey water to complete the ritual.

Follow-Up: At least once a month cover yourself in a clay mask the way the mud people of Papua New Guinea do. Before performing any kind of ritual, they plaster colored earth on their faces to banish negative energy. Clay masks can be purchased in a health food store, or in the cosmetics department of a drug or department store. As the mask hardens, feel it pulling out all the impurities, not only from your skin but from your mind as well. Symbolically rinse it off as a ritual purification.

RITUAL REALITY: My friend Regina's mother was ahead of her time. When Regina, now forty-seven, entered high school, she was one of the youngest students because she had skipped two grades. She was able to keep up with the academics but being a twelve-year-old in a sea of thirteen- and fourteen-year-old freshmen made her feel socially awkward. "There was really nothing I could do to change the situation. My mother knew that the best she could do was make me feel better about myself." Among other suggestions, Regina's mom told her to start taking more baths—not just to cleanse her body, but to relax her and give her time to think. "She told me that before I was born, when my father was in the army, she often felt lonely and frightened. The only thing that eased the anxiety was a hot bath." Her mom took Regina shopping to buy a special body brush and let her pick out a bubble bath scent that appealed to her. She helped Regina set up the room with candles, run the bath to just the right temperature, and then she told her to get into the tub slowly, and just feel the bubbles "caress" her. She also suggested that she imagine that the warmth and water were taking all the stress out of her body.

"I was a little skeptical at first, but I began to look forward to my nightly baths. Somehow, school didn't seem as intimidating after that—I'm not sure why. But I eventually found a little group of friends and felt more comfortable."

Regina has since shared with her own children the relaxing benefits of bathing. And she recognizes that her mother did more than give her a way to cope with social stress. She gave her a gift that lasted a lifetime.

~ Bedtime

SLEEP AND THE DREAMS that come when we enter that wondrous state have always been a subject of great curiosity and fascination. What really happens when we close our eyes, rest our conscious minds, and fall asleep? What are the pictures we see—feelings, fantasies, remembrances? Do they hold keys that unlock the psyche? Do they predict? Warn?

Long before psychologists pondered such questions, earlier cultures came up with their own answers and practices related to sleep. Aboriginal people in Australia concluded that "dream time" is the reality and one's waking life is the dream. Therefore, they go to sleep anticipating a return to what they think of as real life. Native Americans created intricate weblike "dream catchers," so that people could remember their dreams; they are still used today. If you've never seen a dream catcher, it looks like a spiderweb with a hole in the middle, the web for

catching bad dreams, the hole for letting in good dreams. Native Americans also say a prayer to Grandmother Moon before retiring. According to the cabala, the Jewish system of mysticism, when you go to sleep, God takes your soul. Your prayers are a plea to God to allow you to wake up healthy.

Although today we still have not penetrated the mystery of sleep, we know for sure that it is a time for rest and renewal. It only makes sense, then, that a bedtime ritual should help prepare you for the journey, leaving behind all worries and concerns and allowing mind and body to rejuvenate. Most parents naturally do nighttime rituals with their children—for example, one study shows that 86 percent read to their kids at least once a week. Many parents coach their children in a nightly prayer, or climb into bed with their kids just to cuddle.

There is no doubt that a bedtime ritual is clearly one of the sweetest ways of reinforcing the parent/child connection. I offer two here, one for children under ten and another for older children and adults. Feel free to adapt them to include practices you already do and to fit your family's needs.

For Children Under Ten

Intention: To make children feel safe and wind down after their day.
Timing: At bedtime, after all other evening activities and rituals have been done.
Ingredients: Special soap (lavender is calming and good for the skin), and a colored towel reserved for the nighttime cleansing, be it a bath or a quick face wash, a book or story, a bay leaf (protection against nightmares), dream pillow (see below), favorite stuffed animal, or security blanket.

Making a Dream Pillow: A dream pillow is a special pillow filled with herbs to help you sleep and remember your dreams. If your children are old enough to make simple running stitches, you might all make your own dream pillows during a family meeting. Cut two pieces of soft cloth—ideally, something the child has chosen—into a twelve-inch square and stitch together three of the four sides. Into the opening pour a mixture of pleasant-smelling dried herbs, such as lavender (calm), chamomile (restful sleep), rosemary (dream recall), hops (sleep). You might also want to add a small herkimer diamond, a crystal that is good for dream recall. As you sew, think of your action as a ritual, and insert your wishes and dreams with each stitch. (If you are not good at sewing, take a small pillow case, stuff it with herbs, and either ask a friend to help you sew it up or secure the open end with a rubber band.)

Recipe: Give your child at least a fifteen-minute warning before bedtime to help him get ready. A bath ritual before bedtime always facilitates this process because it has a calming effect. At the least, make teeth brushing and face washing part of the preparation for this bedtime ritual. Have the special soap and towel ready. The importance here is consistency—as much as possible, doing the same acts at the same time every evening.

The area around your child's bed should be free of clutter. Before he gets into bed, ceremoniously place the bay leaf under his dream pillow (or you can tie it on a string and hang it over his bed). Use your own words to explain or say, "This tiny little leaf will protect you and keep you safe all night long." As he's about to climb into bed, say something that feels natural and that can be repeated every night. It can be as simple as, "Okay, it's time for you to get in bed," or something unique to your family. Darrel, for instance, says to his daughter Cynthia, "Up and in, my little Cyn!"

Devote a few minutes to talking about the child's day. This is a time when young children are especially good at having conversation, since there are relatively few distractions. If the child talks about her fears or expresses concerns, assure her that sleep will take them away, the dream pillow will bring her good dreams, and that the bay leaf will protect her.

Now it's time for a story. Young children love to hear the same stories over and over again, so have patience. You might also want to sing your child a soothing song or play it on a CD or tape player. As your children get older, let them participate in reading. You read for five minutes and let them read to you for five minutes. Or tell stories with the lights off. This will help them settle down, cuddle up with their favorite toy or object, and get ready for sleep.

The end of this ritual should be some kind of prayer that suits your family traditions. It can be as simple as "God Bless Mommy and Daddy and keep me safe." It can be something that has been passed down in your family. It can be something that the child makes up. Or, it can be a religious prayer that he has learned in Sunday school.

Some parents like to change the order of this ritual, ending with a story, which often puts the child to sleep anyway. That's fine; do whatever works best with your child.

A Cabalistic Prayer

(This prayer can be recited to a child by an adult)

I call on the archangels for protection. May Michael [Divine generosity] protect my right side, Gabriel [the power and strength of God] protect my left side, Uriel [Divine light] be in front of me, and Raphael [healing power] be behind me. I ask God to rest above me and the Shakina [the Divine feminine] to embrace me.

RITUAL REALITIES: Many parents do bedtime rituals with their children. Here is a sampling:

When my son Jourdan had trouble sleeping at age seven, I gave him a Native American dream catcher to hang over his bed. I sprayed his room with lavender and explained that the aroma would help him sleep. When he was nine I began giving him meditation tapes to listen to. It was our little joke when I said, "It's time to plug you in!" All kidding aside, these various calming aids helped him sleep.

Since his son was around three, Tom has been telling Seth, now six, stories in the dark. With the lights off, he's found, Seth moves more easily into sleep. Now that Seth is six, Tom shares the job of storytelling with him. He starts a tale, Seth takes a turn continuing it, and then Tom tells a bit, and so on. Half the time, of course, Seth is deep in dreamland long before the story ever ends.

From the time her son Sasha was two years old, Diane gave him a nightly foot and face massage to calm him down. If by chance she forgot, or told Sasha she was too busy, he protested, "But, Mom, I need you to send me into dreamland!"

Dory reads to her daughter Penny at night. Penny, too, has a dream catcher, and part of their bedtime ritual is to "clean" it out. Every night, Dory holds the dream catcher out Sarah's window and shakes it. "All the bad dreams are out of here, Sarah," she tells her little one. "It's ready for another night of hard work."

For Older Children and Adults

I know many parents who continue bedtime rituals with children well into the teenage years, and they have their own personal bedtime rituals as well. What soothes one teen or adult doesn't necessarily soothe another. Some people, for instance, find that exercising before bed relaxes them, while others get revved up if they exercise at night. Take from this recipe what you think will work best for you.

Intention: To release the day.
Timing: Fifteen minutes before lights out.
Ingredients: Dream pillow (page 58), matches, green candle (healing), sage oil and bowl of warm water or sage leaves (purification), small spiral or looseleaf notebook (approximately five by seven inches), pen or pencil, herbal blend for relaxing (two drops of vetiver, two drops of frankincense, and one drop of orange), diffusor, or small bowl of warm water, herkimer diamond, and small pouch.

Recipe: You first need to transform your bedroom into a place of peace and quiet. You do not want to glance over and see homework or papers from the office, which will make you think of business, so make sure that you have cleared away all work and clutter. If there is a TV in the bedroom, cover the front with a beautiful cloth.

Place your dream pillow on your bed. Sit on

the edge of the bed, and light the green candle. Place a few drops of sage oil in warm water (or burn a small piece of sage in a fireproof bowl). Allow the aroma of the sage to purify your bedroom. While sitting there, take a moment to breath deeply and allow your mind to review the day.

Climb under the covers. Sitting up in bed, use a page in the notebook to write down a list of concerns you have—fear of an upcoming test in school, worry about bills, concern about a relative. When you finish your list, take a deep breath and, as you exhale, release your anxieties to the Divine presence. Tear the paper out of the notebook, rip it or crumble it, and toss it into the trash.

Now place the relaxing herbal blend next to your bed, either in a diffuser or in a bowl of warm water. Start a new page in your notebook. Write down all you have accomplished on this day, no matter how small it may have been. Also list everything you appreciate. If you do this ritual every night, you will toss away your negativity and end up with a notebook that's filled with all your achievements and blessings!

Older children may choose to share their notebooks—or not. This is up to them; teens especially are covetous of their privacy. Likewise, if you are married or living with a significant other, you may want to talk with your partner about your own entries. In any case, try never to go to bed angry—or without telling your loved ones how much you cherish them.

To end this ritual, place a herkimer diamond in a small pouch and put it under your pillow to help you remember your dreams. End with a prayer, the Cabalistic Prayer on page 59, the Evening Prayer below, or something that you and your child or partner write.

Evening Prayer

Mother/Father God, I give thanks for the blessing of this day. Bring me peace and rest so that I may be ready for a new day. I ask for inspiration in my dreams tonight. May I easily remember them when I wake tomorrow.

RITUAL REALITY: When Jason was fourteen, he began having difficulty sleeping. His parents, Matty and Jean, were very concerned, although they figured that much of his anxiety was attributable to adolescence. His body was changing, he seemed more concerned about what his friends said and did, and, not so incidentally, going into ninth grade meant that school was more difficult. Matty, who had been practicing meditation for years, suggested to Jason that he could help him go to sleep every night with a relaxation exercise. Jason was immediately receptive, because over the years his parents had done visualizations with him just for fun. So every night, Matty sat with Jason for a few minutes before bed. He began by asking him to take a few deep breaths. Then he did a progressive relaxation exercise, asking his son to tense and relax his muscles starting at his toes and working up his body. In this very relaxed state, Matty asked Jason to imagine himself in his favorite spot—a beach, a dark forest, a raft in the middle of a gently rocking ocean. Then when he was even more relaxed, Matty asked him to repeat these affirmations: "I am calm, I am safe, and I am falling asleep." After a few weeks of Matty's doing this, Jason surprised him by saying, "I want to try to fall asleep on my own tonight." The next morning, he reported that he had no trouble getting to sleep and slept soundly all night. "I guess I've learned to do my own relaxation," he proudly told his dad.

5. Life Cycle Changes

BEING PART OF A FAMILY means going through constant shifts with one another as well as witnessing family members' individual transitions. Newlyweds become parents, an only child needs to welcome a sibling, an older child enters adolescence. As we struggle to welcome the new and let go of the old, these are at once exciting and tumultuous times . . . which is why we need family life rituals. Ceremonies and rites that honor life cycle changes give families a way to end a particular period or way of being and make room for a new stage, which often carries with it demands for different behavior, increasing responsibilities, and greater privileges. If we don't take time to honor and acknowledge endings and new beginnings, how else can we allow for change and negotiate the future?

Rituals have served this function since the time of the ancients. Many cultures even incorporate symbolic acts such as changing one's appearance to denote moving from one stage to another. In India, Joseph Campbell notes in *The Power of Myth,* when a person passes from one stage of life to another—say, from girlhood to marriage—she changes her attire as well as her name. Likewise, observant Jewish women have to cover their heads after marriage. And there was also a time when a little boy went from short pants to longer trousers, symbolizing that he was able to take on the responsibilities of a man.

Rituals that honor significant life cycle passages, such as becoming a parent, becoming a sibling, or moving into adulthood from childhood, give parents and children a map for living life as socially conscious human beings. They prepare us for the new terrain and acknowledge the skills and tools we need to enter and traverse it. Children, in particular, need this help because, as they grow older and others join the family constellation, the dynamics of the group as a whole begin to change. Children must learn not only appropriate new behaviors that reflect these differences but also skills for interacting with their parents and siblings.

Most important, these rituals help families strengthen their bonds and widen their boundaries. The rituals that follow are meant to be done with all kinds of families—single-parent families, stepfamilies, families with foster children, families with adopted as well as biological children, and people who are considered "kin" through emotional ties. Even more, we are all part of a global family. Therefore, let us teach our children to honor these important passages and show them how they fit not only into generations of their own families but also into the larger scheme of life on our planet.

✑ Becoming a Parent

BECOMING A PARENT is at once a terrifying and exciting prospect for the vast majority of people. Birth parents have nine months to get used to the idea, and adoptive parents also busy themselves in preparation—buying a crib, redecorating a room, picking out a layette. Still, most of us enter parenthood without any rite of passage to mark this incredible and magical transition in our lives.

Interestingly, even the ancient cultures missed the boat on this one. There are few ceremonies specifically designed to honor new parents *together*. Instead, most societies created fertility rituals, often to coincide with a full moon, to promote conception. Others helped prepare a woman (and, less often, a man) to become a parent, encouraging her or him to consciously embody the best qualities of the Divine Mother or the Divine Father—the archetype of ideal parents. In some tribes, medicine men conducted elaborate rituals throughout a woman's preg-

nancy to invite in the spirit child, because it was believed that the soul of the child spoke through the mother or the shaman. The prospective mother spent her nine months walking in nature and listening to the earth for advice and guidance. Most cultures also have birthing rituals, which are geared to lessening the pain of childbirth and protecting mother and child. In ancient Thailand, the figure of a woman is made out of clay, and when the mother goes into labor, its head is decapitated, the idea being that the dangers of childbirth are transferred to the inanimate object. And in the Philippines, the doors and windows are left opened during a woman's labor, to let out the evil spirits.

We have adopted certain aspects of these ancient rites into our own culture. Some people say prayers when a woman goes into labor. And our baby showers are not much different from the Navaho "blessing way" ritual, which honors the mother and is performed approximately a month before the birth. But times have changed. Once solely the province of women, many showers today include the father as well, which reflects our changing times. Nearly 20 percent of all families have a stay-at-home father, so why shouldn't Dad be included in these rituals?

I think we need to go a step further than the baby shower, which in our culture is often more about buying presents for the new arrival than honoring the new parents' passage. When two parents have made the decision to have a child, *both* should be included. I have written the recipe to indicate a mother and a father, both of whom should acknowledge this all-important family transition from partners to parenthood, but the ritual can easily be adapted for a single mother or father or for two parents of the same gender.

Intention: For parents to consciously embrace the qualities of the Divine Mother and Divine Father, and to prepare themselves for the joys and responsibilities of parenthood.

Timing: As close as possible to the time of your baby's birth or, if the child is adopted, to the time of picking up your infant/child.

Ingredients: Matches, two candles—one gold (self-confidence) and one silver (wisdom), small bowl of water, two scarves (or pieces of fabric, approximately twelve by forty-eight inches)—one gold (Divine Father) and one silver (Divine Mother), incense or smudge sticks of sage (purification) and fresh rosemary (forging a strong bond). *Optional (and desirable):* community elders, other family members, and friends; tape recorder or video camera to record the event, food and drink.

Recipe: If possible, the parents-to-be should fast for at least a few hours before the ritual and take a ceremonial bath or shower to purify themselves. Also prepare an altar ahead of time, using a small, low table on which you place the matches, candles, water, sage and rosemary, scarves, and essences.

The prospective parents sit facing each other. If other people are involved, they should form a circle around them. Begin by lighting the candles and explaining their significance. Then light the sage and rosemary and pass it around the circle to purify and sanctify the space. All should take a few moments to breathe the scent into their hearts and invite guidance and support to enter.

The parents should each take a few minutes to think about their apprehensions and concerns about parenthood. This phase of the ritual can take a few minutes or longer, depending on how much time they need.

Now the mother-to-be holds the bowl of water and speaks into it, verbalizing all her fears about being a good mother. For example, she might say, "I release anything that I carry from my past that will keep me from trusting my intuition or inner wisdom. I release my fear that I will not know how to take care of our child. I release my concerns that I will be tired all the time."

The bowl is then passed to the father-to-be, who holds the bowl and releases all his fears and concerns about parenthood into the water. He might say, "I release any misconceptions that keep me from being a loving father. I release all worry and concern that I cannot take care of our child. I release my self-consciousness about being soft and nurturing."

Then the prospective mother and father stand together, both holding the bowl, and ceremoniously throw away the water, keeping in their minds the fact that they are ridding themselves of their apprehension about parenthood. If the ritual is conducted outside, they can simply pour the water into the ground, asking Mother Earth to swallow their fears. Inside, they can go to the sink or toilet and ask God to dispose of their apprehensions.

The mother-to-be now asks her husband and others in the circle to support her in becoming a mother. She may ask her husband to be gentle with her as she makes the transition from being pregnant to becoming a mother. She might ask whomever else is in her circle for child care assistance, hints about mothering, permission to call on them when she needs extra help of any kind.

The father-to-be makes a similar request for support, from his wife and others in the circle. He may ask his wife to truly share parenthood with him and to be patient while he learns to bond with the baby and create his own way of doing things. He may ask the elders in his family to share their wisdom with him. If there are other fathers in the circle, he might ask them to welcome him into their community.

The prospective mother now places the silver cloth around her shoulders as a sign that she is ready to accept the wisdom and take on the energy of the Divine Mother, however she interprets that image based on her own upbringing. By that action, she affirms that she will make a special place in her life for her son or daughter, that she is not alone but rather part of a long tradition of motherhood.

The prospective father places the gold scarf around his shoulders as a sign that he is ready to accept the wisdom and take on the energy of the Divine Father, and that he will find special time when he can be alone with his son or daughter. By doing this, he, too, affirms that he is part of a long tradition of fatherhood.

The ritual ends with a sharing of food and drink and a celebration of this enchanted time of anticipation and hope.

Follow-Up: In the months and years to follow, whenever either of you feels unable to cope with the demands or is insecure about parenthood, place the scarf on your shoulders as a reminder of the support available to you. Also, play the tape or watch the video, if one was made.

RITUAL REALITY: Mara, seven months pregnant when she attended one of my workshops, shared this story with the group: When she turned thirty-five and had no prospects of a husband, she made a courageous and, some believe, controversial decision: to have a child on her own. A successful interior decorator, her hours were up to her and she had both the emotional and financial resources to start her own family. At first, her mother, a widow since Mara was ten, was appalled. Mara explained, "She knew how hard it was to raise a child alone. She was also worried about my grandparents' reaction, what the neighbors would think, and how hard it would be for my child to grow up without a father."

Mara was patient with her mom, among other reasons because some of her concerns were valid. The more they talked, though, and the more Mara's mother told people about her daughter's plan, the more excited she became about having a grandchild. She even accompanied her daughter to have donor insemination. Mara now wanted to do some kind of ritual to commemorate her transition to motherhood.

I told her that all she had to do was adapt my Becoming a Parent ritual to fit her situation. She and her mother planned the whole event, inviting both male and female relatives and friends. They explained that this wasn't a baby shower but rather a celebration of Mara's decision and an affirmation of her future with her child. Guests were asked to bring something that would symbolically show their support.

On the day of the event, everyone sat in a circle around Mara, as she lit the gold and silver candles. Her mother sprinkled salt around the room to purify the space. Mara told her guests not only how difficult it had been for her to make the decision to become a mother but also how much she wanted this child. Her mother then gave Mara an antique shawl that had belonged to her great-grandmother, explaining that it symbolized the wisdom and strength of all the women in the family who had come before

Mara and borne children. Mara then talked about her fears and her desires, and she asked others to support her in her new journey. She asked the women to share their experience; she asked the men to step forth as surrogate dads. One after another, the guests talked about how delighted they were to share in Mara's happiness; they promised they would be there for her emotionally, spiritually, and practically in the months and years to come. They then gave Mara their gifts. The ritual closed with Mara's mother reciting a blessing over her daughter.

Mara's baby, Alicia, is now two years old. Many of the women have helped out when Mara needed to rest or to get out of the house; several of the men have already grown close to Alicia, because they visit often. Mara doesn't feel different from other mothers. "My family may not look like theirs, but I certainly have all the love and support anyone could ask for."

Baby Blessing/Naming

NAMING A BABY blesses him or her and acknowledges that child as a person, a part of the family, and a member of society. Virtually every society and religion have some form of baby-naming or infant-blessing ritual, although the practices differ greatly from culture to culture. These ceremonies are often done on a special day—at the time of a new moon, on the child's actual day of birth, or a certain number of days afterward. These rituals welcome newborns, name them, and protect them.

In ancient Greece, for example, when a baby was five days old, a ceremony was performed to welcome him into the family; his father walked him around the hearth introducing him to Hestia, goddess of the hearth and home, and to the community. In the Catholic Church, and in many cultures, a name is given as soon after the birth as possible. In Asia, a child is given a false name at birth to confuse any evil spirits that want to steal him. In St. Lucia, when a child is four or five years old, she is given a special coconut tree, considered her tree of life; her umbilical cord, which has been saved since birth, is buried under its roots.

While we tend to pore over baby books to find suitable names, ancient cultures often turned to religious customs or trusted their spiritual guides, priests, and even fortune-tellers to make such decisions, because they believed that names carried with them great power. In some primitive cultures, the shaman goes into meditation and prayer and receives the soul name of the child. In certain tribes in Africa, a ceremony is performed, during which the pregnant woman is put into trance so that she can connect to the soul of the child and in that way learn his or her name. Ashkenazi (Eastern European) Jews believe that a child should not be named after a living relative because it would rob a person of his full life if another member of the family were to carry his name in his lifetime. Therefore, children are named after relatives who have passed on to Spirit.

In many cultures, children are given two names, a spiritual name and a legal one that will be used in everyday life. Catholics give their children a saint's name that is sanctified during baptism. In Bali, where there is a caste system, a child's name indicates his or her station in life as well as sequence of birth—for instance, all firstborns in the lower caste are called "Wayan"; they are named "Gede" or "Putu" in the upper castes.

Although baby-naming ceremonies traditionally take place in a church or temple, these rituals were once held outdoors, near a tree that stood for the tree of life. For instance, in ancient Israel, a cedar tree was planted for the birth of a new boy and a cypress tree was planted for a new girl. The growing children cared for "their" trees and, eventually, married under a canopy made of branches cut from each partner's tree. For this ritual, I have adapted the use of a tree, because I feel it is a wonderful symbol of strength and rootedness. It can be done with a biological or an adopted child (see also Gotcha Day to celebrate an adopted child's arrival, page 96).

Intention: To welcome a new child into the world and to introduce her/him to the community.

Timing: Depending on your personal, religious, or cultural convictions, anywhere from a few days to a month after the birth or adoption. (If you have adopted an older child and have changed or added to her name, you can do this ritual at any time.)

Ingredients: A large houseplant or a tree (one already in your backyard that you designate for your child or a new one which you will plant), cornmeal (nourishment), smudge stick, matches, pillow (big enough to hold the baby), bowl of water, rose (love), rosemary (long life), basil (mental clarity), orange (joy), a white gown for the baby (purity), cardboard tags with holes, string, helium balloons, musical instruments or a tape/CD player and your favorite family music (if your child is adopted from another country or culture, it's a good idea to play a tape or CD that evokes those roots), pens and pencils.

Recipe: If you are city dwellers, this ritual can be done indoors with a potted tree that you can keep in your home or later transplant to a spot outdoors. Whether you do this indoors or out, create an altar (page 30) around the tree, placing at its base the cornmeal, the pillow, the water, rose, rosemary, basil, and the orange.

This should be a joyous occasion, so invite many family members and friends to celebrate with you. At least one person should be designated Guardian, or, if you prefer the term, Godparent. The oldest present is considered the Elder. Have everyone stand in a circle around the foot of the tree. The mother holds the infant, wearing the white gown, and the father puts his arm around the mother, signifying an unbroken family bond. (If there are other children, they, too, should be part of this chain.) Lighting a smudge stick of sage, the Guardian will first purify the area to create sacred space. This tree is now designated as the baby's tree and connected to the universal Tree of Life.

The Elder begins with a prayer to the Divine, requesting protection for the child. She can use the Baby Blessing below, make up one of her own, or use one that reflects your family's particular spiritual practice.

Baby Blessing

(Use the appropriate gender pronouns)

Great God of Light, we ask that this child be blessed and protected.
May she know herself as a radiant child of God.
May her heart remain open and loving so she may give and receive abundant love.
May she know compassion.

May she never want for food or shelter.
May happiness surround her all the days of her life.

The child's mother places him on the pillow at the base of the tree. She then holds up the bowl of water and says a prayer for the baby to be emotionally healthy. *("May God give you the courage and calm to withstand the stresses of life and the wisdom to make good decisions.")* She then washes the baby's feet as a symbol that she will nurture and care for him.

Now the child's father takes a few grains of cornmeal and sprinkles it around the tree, offering his prayers that the baby be taken care of physically. *("May God grant you strength and courage, for all that you must do.")*

The Guardian lights a candle and prays for the child to be guided and connected to Spirit. *("May God watch over you, and may you always be in touch with your inner guidance.")*

All present now write their wishes for the child on the cardboard tags. Allow even young children to participate; if they cannot write, they can draw pictures that represent their wishes for the new arrival on the tags (or even just scribble on them—it's the sentiments that count).

The Elder now holds up the child, and

announces her name. If the child also has been given a spiritual name, it is whispered to her. The Elder begins to turn slowly, reciting the child's name four times to each of the four directions: to the *east* for clarity, new beginnings, and pure thoughts; to the *south* for passion and compassion; to the *west* for deep feelings and intuition; to the *north* for foundation, abundance, and a healthy body.

The participants now tie their tags of good wishes onto the balloons and let them fly outside, symbolically sending their prayers to Spirit. Music is played and food is shared in celebration of the new life and the new member of the community.

Follow-Up: Whatever music has been chosen for this ritual—a particular song or classical piece—can be played annually on the child's Birthday Ritual (page 91) or, if he's adopted, on Gotcha Day (page 96).

RITUAL REALITY: Henry and Carolyn had been trying to have a child for five years. Imagine their delight when Carolyn became pregnant and, after an ultrasound test, learned she was carrying twin boys, due to arrive in July. Each of the prospective parents had lost one of their own parents recently, so they decided that one boy would be named Patrick after Carolyn's mother, Patricia, and the other Michael, after Henry's dad. Having known Carolyn since high school, I was honored when she asked me to perform a ceremony to name and bless their sons.

I followed the recipe above, but what made this occasion even more special was its connection to generations past. The ceremony, which took place a week after the boys' arrival, was held at Carolyn's family's summer home in Long Island, which had been in her family for years; she and her cousins had practically grown up there. On the grounds was a little chapel where Henry and Carolyn had been married and where generations of Boyles had gathered for prayer and other special occasions. The boys wore white christening gowns that had been passed down in Henry's family. His mom and Carolyn's dad were the Elders (it's okay to have more than one, especially when there are twins), and Henry's oldest sister, who had six children of her own, was the Guardian. When the Elders held the boys up and announced their names, there wasn't a dry eye in the crowd.

"I felt as if our parents were here with us," Carolyn later told me. Remembering her mother, a vibrant woman who never missed a school play, even if Carolyn was only a tree, I was sure they were.

Becoming a Sibling

WE HEAR A GREAT deal about "sibling rivalry," but a lot less about sibling devotion and connection, and yet this is one of the most sacred of all family bonds. Our sisters and brothers know us as few others do; they can be our role models, our best friends, and our tormentors. They can teach us by example, or by taking us in hand. Because of our siblings, we learn what loyalty and caring feel like and what relationships mean. And forever after in life, we look for—or avoid—certain qualities that remind us of our brothers and sisters.

Ancient cultures stressed not only the joys of being a sibling but also the responsibilities. In Egypt, the brother/sister bond was considered so sacred that the Pharaohs married their sisters, and the two ruled together. In other cultures, the order of siblings determined their role in life: Firstborn sons inherited the land; second born were warriors; and third born were marked for the priesthood. Even today, in India, Rakhi Day is a full moon commemoration of Lord Varuna, deity of water. It is a time when *rakhis* (bracelets) are given for protection—by sisters to their brothers.

Although we often take pains to prepare children for the arrival of a sibling, we don't have ceremonies for them to mark this important life passage. I've adopted a little bit of this and that for this simple honoring of siblinghood. It can be done with one child, or if the new arrival is last in a long line of children, with several older siblings.

Intention: For the older child(ren) to honor and celebrate siblinghood and to find his/her place in the family tree.

Timing: Preparation begins when you tell your child(ren) you are pregnant; the ceremony itself takes place after the birth of the baby.

Making a Protection Mobile: In the months leading up to the birth of the sibling, have your child(ren) help with the construction of a protection mobile, or make one on his own. Encourage him to decorate it with bits of colorful paper, shiny stones, and words that denote prayers of protection ("health," "safety," "pleasant dreams," and so on). Use age-appropriate supplies—pipe cleaners to wire hangers, nontoxic paint, cardboard cutouts, pictures from magazines. Put pictures of the family on it so the baby can look up and see the family overhead. If there is more than one older child, you might have them work together or have each child make his own mobile—there's no such thing as too much protection!

Recipe: Begin preparing the child(ren) when you announce that you are pregnant. Young children need to know that they will still be important and loved when the baby arrives. Even in small ways, let them participate in the decorating of the room and the changing configuration of space within the household. This may be a time when an older child moves from a crib to a grown-up bed, or gets a new blanket or something else to represent her changing status. Ask the older child's permission to use her old infant seat, bottles, or baby clothes, and thank her for being so generous toward her new sibling.

Also make time to create a family tree. Using a large piece of poster board, or cardboard cut from the side of a carton, paste pictures of family members in the configuration of a family tree. Grandparents go on top with arrows to the row below, which shows their children (you and your siblings—your children's aunts and uncles). From your photos, draw arrows to the next row below, pointing to your child(ren) and to a blank square in which you write "reserved"—for the new baby.

On the day that the new brother or sister comes home from the hospital, have the family tree poster ready along with a first snapshot of the new baby. Allow the children to paste in the baby's picture and to draw the word *sister* or *brother* under their own names. If they are too young, write it for them. Before the new baby even enters her room (which might also be the older child's room), ask the sibling(s) to hang the protection mobile, either over the new arrival's crib or at the entrance to the room. It is important for older children to feel that they are participating in welcoming the new baby and giving her this first gift.

Finally, place the pendant around the child's neck and say, "You are now [sister/brother] of [name of the baby]. You can receive love from [baby's name] as well as give love to [her/him]. Just as you have given your new sibling a gift of protection, I give you this pendant, which will help you be strong, caring, and safe."

One or both parents, if possible, should then take the older sibling(s) out for a special celebration without the baby.

Follow–Up: Mark the date, and every year take the older sibling(s) out to celebrate Sister/Brother Day.

RITUAL REALITY: When Ariana was three, her parents told her she was going to become a sister. To prepare her, they gave her a life-size doll and taught her to diaper and feed a baby. They bought Ariana a "big girl's bed," let her pick out her first set of sheets, and held a special ceremony during Mom's eighth month to mark Ariana's move into her new bed. They also asked her to think of and make special

snacks that they could keep on the bottom of the refrigerator where she could reach without anyone's assistance. Each of these steps made Ariana feel special and, just as important, more independent as well. Since her parents already knew the baby's gender (Mom had had an amnio), they were even able to include their firstborn in the fun of picking out a name for her new brother. Of all the choices, "Scott" was Ariana's favorite, so Scott it would be.

Ariana's parents used a houseplant to make a family tree. On its leaves, they attached snapshots of the family, and on one of the lower branches, a blank piece of paper. They told Ariana that when the new baby arrived, she could clip his picture on that branch.

Mom and Dad also told Ariana that they needed her help in preparing Max, their Border collie, for the new baby, because they were afraid he'd feel left out. (With young children, this technique—talking about the fears or resentments of a pet, a doll, or a character in a book—often makes it easier for children to express their own feelings.) As it turned out, Max did seem apprehensive. The minute the new crib was assembled, he sensed that something different was happening at home. He began sleeping under the new crib. Noticing his new behavior, Ariana told her parents that she didn't want Max to be scared at night, so she put some of his toys under the crib. When Scott arrived, Dad brought home the stuffed animal that the hospital had given Scott and gave it to Ariana, telling her it was from her new baby brother. They gave Max a blanket from the hospital, and explained to Ariana that it would help Max get used to the baby's smell.

A day later, when Ariana's parents brought Scott home, Grandma and Grandpa were invited to witness Ariana's sibling ceremony. Her parents lit a candle, and said, "This is in honor of Sister Day." They gave her the Polaroid of Scott in the hospital nursery and helped her affix it to the branch on the family tree reserved for him. Then they let Ariana blow out the candle. Afterward, Grandma and Grandpa had the joy of baby-sitting for their new grandson, and Ariana had Mom and Dad all to herself. She had a "big girl's dinner" at a nearby restaurant, where, her parents told her, babies weren't allowed. They also gave her a tiny ID bracelet that said "Ariana" on one side, and "Big Sister" on the other. Even though she couldn't read the words, Ariana knew what the letters stood for, and she wore her bracelet like a medal of honor in the weeks that followed. She delighted in introducing her new brother to visitors and showing them where she and Scott fit in on the family tree.

~ Puberty: The Passage to Adulthood

PUBERTY, by definition, is the age at which a person is first capable of reproduction. In common law, it is presumed to be age fourteen for boys, twelve for girls. It is associated with certain physical changes—deepening of the voice, body and facial hair in boys; menstruation, pubic hair, and a softening of the body in girls. But, of course, puberty is so much more: an invitation to adulthood and a time when a young woman or man is welcomed into a new phase of life that brings with it not only physical change but emotional and social responsibilities.

In fact, from the dawn of humankind, societies have created rituals to honor a child's passage into adulthood. For girls, these rites typically focus on menstruation. Native Americans girls are honored by being initiated into the Moon Lodge at the time of their first bleeding. The Cherokees believe that a tribe's fertility is its lifeblood, so a girl's entering "moontime" is a blessed event, and bleeding is associated with

power. In many cultures, a menstruating women is not allowed to participate in tribal ceremonies. Rather, she is encouraged to meditate and pray and to listen to her dreams, because psychic abilities are allegedly strongest at this time. In fact, some societies consider a menstruating woman powerful enough to heal the sick or even to bring on the rain.

In ancient times, when lives were closely linked with nature and people followed the moon calendar, tribal sisters often bled at the same time. (We see this same phenomenon today in college dorms, especially among close friends.) Ancient Israelite women celebrated their moontime in a separate tent. Freed from the daily responsibilities, they shared stories, recipes, herbs, and songs, and used this time for rest and restoration. Sadly, we have lost most of these traditions in modern times. In contrast, we unwittingly condition our daughters to dread this time of month, and to view their cramps and bloated stomachs as "the curse" our mothers once described.

We also can find ancient and modern initiation rites for boys in almost every culture. Many of the older customs that herald manhood include circumcision or ritual scarring of the body, in conjunction with a so-called vision quest during which the boy braves the elements and asks the gods for guidance. When a boy returns from such ordeals, he is considered a man. With his new status come additional responsibilities and traits, such as strength and courage. The Sufis in Turkey, as well as tribes in Africa, continue to celebrate puberty in mass circumcision rites, somewhere between ages ten and twelve, depending on the boys' maturity. Afterward, the boys—now considered men—run through the streets so that the community might embrace them and their new role in society. In many cultures, these rites also involve a symbolic separation from the mother. When a Hindu boy turns seven, for instance, his mother makes a sacrifice at the temple, donating a piece of jewelry or some other object of value, as a token of her letting go. She does this for many years, allowing herself and her son to get used to the idea of separation; when the boy reaches puberty, a ceremony honoring his manhood is finally performed.

We see echoes of these traditions in modern religious rituals as well. The Catholic Church confers a new name on a boy or girl during con-firmation, typically age twelve or thirteen. In Judaism, a thirteen-year-old boy has a Bar Mitzvah to commemorate his manhood, a girl a Bat Mitzvah. In both faiths, family and members of the community join in the celebrations. But do these ceremonies really mark adulthood for our sons and daughters?

In our culture, the journey to maturity is prolonged way past the teen years, so when does a girl become a woman? Her first date? When she loses her virginity? When she can earn money? When she becomes a mother? Though young women nowadays have confirmation rites and sweet-sixteen parties, such practices don't really honor the meaning of these life transitions, nor do they incorporate elder guidance as the ancient rituals did. Likewise, we might ask, when does a boy really become a man? When is he considered a responsible member of the community? When he gets his driver's license? His first job? When he joins the army? Or when he marries and fathers a child? He and his family may celebrate "manhood" in a religious ceremony, or perhaps he pierces his ear or gets tattooed as a show of independence, but these rites don't compare to ancient rituals that truly marked this important life-stage transition.

Many mothers and fathers today, particularly those who see themselves as part of larger spiritual communities, and have educated themselves about the rituals of other cultures, want more for their daughters and sons. Some call me to ask if I'll help them adapt the ancient rituals. The problem is, because the culture at large hasn't caught up with this new consciousness, the children of these enlightened parents think it's "weird" or "geeky" to honor these passages. Girls often feel self-conscious celebrating the onset of their periods. Boys are embarrassed when fathers suggest a vision quest or, even worse, urge them to be expressive and vulnerable in front of their friends. Although many of these girls and boys are increasingly exposed to adult issues and are even beginning to mature physically at earlier and earlier ages, they often lack the emotional maturity to handle more elaborate puberty rites.

Therefore, I offer two types of puberty rituals: the first a simple one that honors the physical changes of early puberty and is done in the pre-teen years; the second a more involved initiation ceremony designed to help a teenager embrace the social and emotional responsibilities of adulthood, ideally involving other family members and friends.

According to the Belgian anthropologist Arnold van Gennep, many initiation rituals have a common structure: a period of separation when the young person is cut off from his former role, a time of transition from one state to another, and then a reentry into the tribe with new status. Often an educational element is included, whereby the young person learns from the elders a new skill or different behavior. In Alaska, a young man is taught to kill his first seal; in India, a young woman learns to milk her first buffalo. Traditionally, the teachings involved in male and female initiation rites have reflected the differences between men's and women's roles. However, I have tried to combine the best of both worlds, because I believe that our children need to be prepared for *all* roles. Our daughters need courage and adventure in their lives; our sons need sensitivity and vulnerability. Both are partners in procreation; and both should be responsible for the hunt *and* the hearth.

Select from these rituals what you think will work best for your child. Doing rituals with teenagers is a lot like trying to talk to them. If you've made ritual a part of your family life all along and if you've kept the lines of communication open, your child will be receptive to these types of celebration and enjoy participating in them. If you haven't, chances are you'll encounter some resistance. Under no circumstances should you force a kid to do either ritual. Remember, too, that these rituals are as much for the parents as for the kid, to acknowledge a child's increasing physical and emotional maturity and to accept her need for separation, which is a natural part of adolescence. We ought to take our clues from the Hindus, and start the process early. By *gradually* acknowledging our children's growth, both they and we will be better prepared for their adulthood. And we will not only have different expectations for them, we will also treat them differently than we did when they were children.

Early Puberty

Intention: To mark the physical onset of puberty.

Timing: Typically when a youngster is anywhere from eleven to fourteen and beginning to show *physiological* signs of change—for a girl, her first period, for a boy, facial hair or a deepening of his voice.

Ingredients: Carnelian (self-esteem, sexuality), moonstone for a girl (acknowledging the changing cycles) or gold for a boy (courage and confidence), leather or chamois pouch, a symbolic article from an older relative—a book, tool, piece of jewelry, handkerchief or other article of clothing that represents generations past who have made this same passage.

Recipe: In the years leading up to puberty, long before there is any evidence of physical change, talk to your child about puberty—what it is, how his or her body will change, and why. Also discuss the emotions and new responsibilities that come with having a more grown-up body. The more at ease your son or daughter is about these changes, and the more he or she understands, the less self-conscious both of you will be.

When your child starts showing the physical signs of change, Dad should make a date with his son, Mom with her daughter. Explain that to celebrate those changes you'd like to go somewhere special or engage in an adult activity of the child's choosing—a favored sporting event, a concert, a pleasurable experience such as a massage, hunting, fishing, even get the child's ears pierced! Then go out for a special lunch or dinner to discuss what this change means: new privileges, such as a slightly later curfew, additional allowance, the right to stay home alone when parents go out; new responsibilities, such as being in charge of dinner once a week or helping with younger siblings. You'll have to determine the specifics based on your values, the nature of your family, and your child's capabilities.

To seal the pact, give your preteen a "power pouch" with a piece of carnelian to symbolize emerging sexuality and respect for one's body. For a girl, you can add a moonstone; for a boy, you can add a piece of gold (such as a coin or amulet). You can also add other symbolic items and stones of your own choosing that are particularly suited to your child. The pouch can be kept in a drawer, a backpack, or worn around the neck.

To end the ritual, give him or her an item that belonged to an older relative of the same gender—for a girl, something that belonged to your mother, grandmother, or a favorite aunt; for a boy, something that belonged to your father, grandfather, or favorite uncle. And, in whatever words you are comfortable using, tell the child that the gift symbolizes the generations before him or her who have made this important passage from child to adult. The item should serve as a reminder of both the power and the responsibility of this new stage of life.

Follow-Up: In the weeks that follow, the parent of the opposite sex should take the child out for special grown-up time, too. If the child is self-conscious about the changes, don't overdo the event. Show by your actions that you intend to treat the preteen differently or say something understated, such as, "I know your mom/dad took you out to celebrate your new status in the family. This is my way of telling you I recognize the difference, too."

RITUAL REALITIES:

     ⌒ When her daughter, Amy, called from school to say that she had cramps and was bleeding for the first time, Sarah, who was ready for this very moment, drove to school to pick up her daughter. Once they reached the car, safely out of view of friends and teachers, Sarah gave Amy a single red rose as a symbol of her new status as a woman and a crocheted bag in which to keep her sanitary products. When they arrived home, Amy was delighted to find that her mother had also made a tent in her room, using a sheet and two strait chairs, inside of which she had placed a nest of pillows. "I remember how much you liked to hide in a tent when you were little," Sarah explained. "Well, you're obviously not a little girl anymore, but that doesn't mean you can't retreat to a special place." She gave her daughter some hot tea to ease her cramps and a journal to record her first feelings of womanhood.

With the changing configurations of families today, especially given the large number of households headed by single parents, there isn't always a mother in the house to honor her daughter's first period or a dad to celebrate with his son. Several families I know have adapted this ritual to suit their needs:

     ⌒ Kyle and his wife, Freda, separated when their daughter Susie was ten. Although they co-parented, alternating weekends with their daughter, both parents agreed that it was best for Susie to spend weeknights with Kyle, because he worked at home. A year later, Freda's company transferred her overseas for six months, so Kyle became the primary caretaker, with Susie spending school holidays and summer vacations in France with her mother. Kyle had always been a hands-on dad, but the separation caused him to broaden his roles even more. He taught Susie how to cook and sew; and he took an interest in her Barbie collection and listened patiently when she talked about problems with her girlfriends. Not surprisingly, because they also talked about the facts of life, Susie came to him when she got her first period. He didn't make a big deal of it, because he was afraid to embarrass her, but the next day, when Susie came home from school, Kyle presented her with a bouquet of red roses, and invited her to a special candlelit "tea" he had prepared for her. He gave her a silver heart-shaped pendant that had belonged to his mother. "This was Grandma's, and now you should have it to mark the beginning of your journey toward womanhood."

ℰↄ Bethany, a single mother, was concerned when she began to notice the peach fuzz darkening on her son Mark's chin. Realizing she could never substitute for Mark's father, who had died when the boy was ten, she asked her brother, Stewart, if he'd help. Stewart made a date with Mark every other weekend to do some "guy stuff" without Mom, and the more time they spent together, the more easily Mark opened up and began asking questions about the changes in his body. Meanwhile, Bethany didn't want to act as if she didn't notice what was going on, so she started treating Mark differently. She taught him how to carve a turkey. She allowed him to open a bank account in his own name. And when Mark complained that he was "too old" to go to his pediatrician, she allowed him to switch to the family doctor, admitting that since he was getting older, that was a great idea. In fact, it would be up to him to make the appointments on his own and to ride his bicycle to his checkups. However, if any important decisions about his health needed to be made, she wanted Mark to know that the doctor would call her, too. Not surprisingly, Mark responded by becoming more responsible than ever. Sensing that Bethany was not only letting go, but also placing more faith in his judgment, he took his new status in the family very seriously and, paradoxically, felt closer to his mom than he ever had felt before.

Initiation to Adulthood

Intention: To mark a young person's entry into adulthood and to welcome him or her into the larger community.

Timing: Anywhere from age thirteen through sixteen, or even older, depending on the teenager's maturity and comfort level.

Ingredients: Sleeping bag, tent, and other camping equipment, a white twenty-four-hour candle in a glass (the innocence of childhood), matches, essence of sage (purification), power animal (to be chosen by the initiate), journal or notebook and pen, wooden box (with paints, markers, glue, and other materials for decoration), gold and silver candles (masculine and feminine energies), pine or cedar (grounding and connection to the earth), daffodil oil or flower (new beginnings), geranium (happiness and protection), medicine pouch (to be filled with crystals and gemstones donated by members of the family and friends), large piece of poster board, bowl filled with green (harmony) finger paint or washable tempera paint. *For a girl:* red wine or grape juice (menstrual blood and other feminine strengths), a shawl bought specifically for this occasion. *For a boy:* white wine or white grape juice (semen and other masculine strengths), a vest bought specifically for this occasion.

Recipe: This ritual is somewhat involved, so start planning and preparation at least a month ahead. To friends and relatives who will participate, send invitations with instructions or call to explain the ritual. You can make this an all-female affair for a daughter, all-male for a son, or mix genders. Either way, be sure the guests understand that they're to come prepared with three things: a crystal or gemstone symbolizing a quality they would like to bestow upon the teen; a story about their own initiation into adulthood—something surprising, frightening, wonderful; and a favorite food to share at the end of the ceremony.

Also prepare the teenager for the ritual, explaining everything that is going to take place. Make sure he is comfortable with the ceremony. The amount of detail you offer depends on the teen. You may want to explain everything or surprise him with certain elements of it, preparing him in general terms only ("a special ceremony that will honor your transition to adulthood"). Either way, have him choose a power animal as a spirit guide; use a statue, picture, or Animal Medicine Card (see pages 20–21) to represent that creature. You might want to involve the teen in the making of or shopping for a ceremonial vest or shawl.

The first part of the ritual, conducted on the night before the actual ceremony by a parent or another relative of the same gender, involves the young person going into nature to spend time alone, contemplating his initiation. (If weather doesn't permit this, a tent can be set up indoors.) Inside the tent, have ready the white candle, matches, sage oil, an object symbolizing the teen's chosen power animal, journal and pen, and the wooden box with materials for decoration. The ceremony, which will involve other relatives and friends, will take place the next morning and will end with a feast of celebration. Both for safety's sake and convenience, some adult participants might want to camp out near the teenager; this should be discussed and weighed beforehand.

To begin, the mother of the girl or the father of the boy will light the white twenty-four-hour candle as a symbol of childhood and then purify the tent with essence of sage by putting a few drops of the oil in water and sprinkling it around the area. (Be sure to position the candle safely.) Then Mother/Father will escort the teen into the initiation tent, explaining that the candle will burn throughout the night to represent his last day as a child. Ask the teen to meditate about where he is in his life. He can think about the qualities he has chosen in his power animal and imagine them in himself—the leadership qualities of a lion, the broad perspective of the eagle, or the joy of the hummingbird. Depending on the teen's previous experience with meditation, the parent might want to lead him in a guided meditation to jump-start the process of introspection.

Before leaving the teen, explain that she will use her time alone for further contemplation, to write her thoughts in the new journal, and to use the materials in the tent, as well as objects she finds in nature, to turn the ordinary wooden box into an initiation box that commemorates her new status. She might use leaves or flowers, stones or feathers. (If the ritual is done inside, she can cut pictures out of magazines.) Encourage her to use her intuition, both to come up with words or symbols that she might paint on the outside of the box, and to choose artifacts, such as her animal guide, that she'll keep inside the box. Stress that there's no right or wrong way to do this; she should just go with her feelings.

The next morning, the teen is not to come out of the tent until one of the elders—ideally, the oldest one present—invites her to join their circle. She brings the white candle with her, which by now has burned low. Inside the circle will be an altar containing the silver and gold candles, the pine (or cedar), the daffodil and geranium. She sits next to the altar, surrounded by the community. In unison, those in the circle say, "We welcome you into the community of adults." The teen blows out the white candle as a symbol of leaving her childhood, and the Elder lights the gold and silver candles, explaining that the two colors represent masculinity and femininity. To be a whole person, we all must embody both sides. The Elder points out that the pine (or cedar) is so that the teen will always feel grounded and connected to nature, the daffodil symbolizes the beginning of a new stage in her life, and the geranium her future happiness and protection.

The mother/father of the teen helps her/him into the shawl/vest, which denotes new status in the community, and recites a special blessing that she/he has written for this ceremony. Parents should be sure that the blessing addresses all the qualities they want the young person to possess, including nontraditional ones, such as sensitivity for a boy, and courage for a girl.

The teen then states his own commitment to maturity, responsibility, and service, making a specific commitment to do something to give back to the community—for example, work in a soup kitchen, plant a tree, help an elderly person, volunteer at the community center.

The Elder gives the teen the empty medicine pouch, explaining that members of the community will fill it with blessings. As the young person walks around the circle, each member of the community touches his forehead and gives him a crystal or gemstone, explaining what quality it represents—say, an amethyst for spiritual awareness, a topaz for new beginnings, a tiger's eye for courage. Each person also talks about what becoming an adult meant to him or her.

After the medicine pouch has been filled, the teen holds up the large piece of poster board, dips his hands in the washable green paint, and leaves a hand print in the center, after which everyone else follows suit. He is then officially considered an adult in the community, his hand one of many that works in harmony with others. The Elder closes the ceremony with a wine or grape juice toast to the new adult and to the feeling of togetherness within the community, and the feast begins, with everyone symbolically sharing the initiation.

Follow-Up: The new adult should hang the hand print poster in her room as a reminder that she is one part of a larger whole. She can wear the shawl (or vest) for other rituals, or put it on whenever extra courage or insight is needed.

RITUAL REALITY: I have found that adolescence is stretched out longer and longer these days. So, while some "puberty" rituals correspond with the biological event, many happen much later. For example, Yolanda, a divorced mother of two, went through a tumultuous adolescence with her younger child, Bart, a troubled teen who struggled throughout most of his school years, getting kicked out of several high schools. A proper diagnosis—ADD—and the right kind of help, which involved Bart's going on medication for a short time and, more important, going to a special school, finally changed the young man's downhill course, although it took him seven long years to get through college. Yolanda marveled as she watched her once recalcitrant teen become mature. Bart was twenty-five when he graduated, and at that point Yolanda knew her son had finally grown up. "I wanted him to know how special I thought the achievement was and to recognize how hard he had struggled to get there." So on graduation weekend, Yolanda prepared a private ritual for the two of them. She lit a blue candle for clarity and trust, and told him how proud she was of his achievements. She gave him a green pouch for abundance, and inside it were small stones and other items representing qualities she thought he'd need in his new life: an amethyst for spiritual awareness, fluorite for releasing unwanted energies, a tourmaline for balance, a rose quartz for love, a few black peppercorns for courage, a tiny gold bird representing self-confidence and the freedom to soar as high as he dared. It wasn't lost on Bart that his mother was finally letting go of her fears for him as well!

6. Family Days

A COMMON NOTION of family is based on what we believe it was like to live in the "good old days," when everyone sat around the dinner table or the fire, talking, laughing, and playing games. Kids learned adult skills from their parents, often working with grown-ups to get the land tilled, the animals fed, and the household chores done. Naturally, families held celebrations, such as christenings and weddings, but being together wasn't much of a novelty, because adults and children spent so much time together, working toward common goals.

This romantic, and perhaps idealized, image of "old days" may not be accurate. But we know for sure that any kind of togetherness is rare nowadays. Families tend to have complicated arrangements as the adults and children go their separate ways to conduct the business of their complex lives. Because we are all so busy and we spend less time than we'd like with our children, celebrating special family days is more important than ever. Commemorating these times brings family members closer to one another in the present and, at the same time, connects them to their roots in the past. Moreover, in this kid-centered world of ours, children rarely take the time to do something special *for* their parents (or grandparents). Rituals, however, remind children to honor the older generation. They also help them develop respect for Mother Earth, and the Divine Spirit in all things.

You probably already include birthday parties, anniversary dinners, and standard holidays, such as Mother's Day or Father's Day, in your family repertoire. Most of us do. And some families develop rituals unique to their family. For instance, one family I know has "restaurant night," when everyone gets dressed up, and the men in the family, Dad and his eleven-year-old son, cook for the women. A divorced mother has "pig night" once a month—a dinner where the kids don't have to use utensils.

If you're already celebrating the typical family holidays, keep it up. But because these kinds of traditions are so important, you also might want to create new ritual celebrations that meet the unique needs of today's families—times when we say to members of our family, "You are important." Try the ones I suggest in this chapter, or make up your own.

Birthday Ritual

ALTHOUGH the ancient Greeks believed that candles—a precursor of our own birthday custom—were magical and had the power to grant wishes, celebrating birthdays is a fairly new phenomenon in modern culture. Once, in fact, the "birth day" was acknowledged only by royalty. In part, this is because no birth records were kept for common people. On this special day, the royal was surrounded by giant candles, which were supposed to bring in Spirit and convey good fortune upon the celebrant.

Today, it's hard to find a family that doesn't celebrate birthdays! But in our frenzy to have fun, we sometimes forget to look at what each passing year means. I certainly don't suggest that we do away with birthday bashes, or that we stop blowing out candles on the cake. But why not add new experiences to this popular rite and touch upon the deeper issues that come with each passing year?

As psychologists Evan Ember-Black and Janine Roberts point out in *Rituals for Our Time,* "Birthdays are good markers of developmental changes in family, as children pass through childhood, the teenage years, and into adulthood." We need only look at the kinds of birthday parties we give to see this phenomenon: cake, party favors, fun and games for little kids; a pizza or bowling party for teens; a night on the town for adults. Parents are usually front and center at their offspring's first birthday party—in fact, they tend to enjoy the party more than the child does; ten years later, most children prefer that Mom and Dad make themselves scarce!

The following birthday ritual, which literally spans the entire "birth day," can be done in addition to whatever kind of traditional birthday party you plan. It brings in elements that help a child (or adult) see himself in the larger scheme of his own life and his family.

Intention: To celebrate the anniversary of one's birth and to encourage introspection about how the celebrant, no matter how young or old, can contribute to his own growth and to the greater human good.

Timing: The day of the birthday, starting when the child or adult wakes up.

Ingredients: Seeds, bulb or young plant, trowel for planting, plant marker or homemade sign, bowl of salt water (purification) and towel, an item the person wants to give away, an item that represents the coming year in the person's life, birthday book (see below), cake (flavor chosen by celebrant), birthday candles, balloon filled with sweets. Indoors: potting soil and pot.

Creating a Birthday Book: Put a photograph of the birthday person on the front cover of a large book with blank pages or an album. In the weeks before the birthday, when you invite family and friends to this ritual, ask everyone to bring thoughts, poems, or a symbol that can be pasted into the birthday book—a compilation of anything people love and want to share with the celebrant.

Recipe: Begin the day by acknowledging that this is the person's special day. He is exempt from all chores and other responsibilities. Start with his favorite breakfast. It's fun, too, to have surprise decorations in his room (done while he's sleeping) and throughout the house. After breakfast, suggest that he pick out something that he's never done before—depending on his age and maturity, cross the street for the first time, or go to the mall, drive the family car, or, in the case of an adult, do something pleasurable that he's never allowed himself to do.

Later in the day, when the guests have arrived, begin the ritual with a tree-planting ceremony—ideally outside. If weather doesn't permit, or if you're a city dweller, you can also do this inside with seeds, a bulb, or a small houseplant. Have everyone gather in a circle, holding hands. Explain that you'll all take a moment to breathe deeply and make this a sacred space. Envision white light surrounding the area and silently say a blessing for the birthday person. Stress that this ritual planting is not only to mark the passage of his own life by witnessing the growth of this seedling but also for him to learn about his responsibility toward the earth and all of the life it gives.

Have each guest take a turn removing a shovelful of dirt from the ground; or, if indoors, let everyone take a tiny handful of potting soil and add it to a large pot into which the seeds, bulb, or young plant will be placed. When the ground (or pot) is ready, the celebrant will come forth and do the planting. If it's a child's birth-

92

day, knowledgeable adults can make sure the bulb is right side up, or that the dirt is properly tamped around the new growth. Place the small sign next to the plant: "Jonathan, age 5, 1999." The person is now responsible for the care and nurturing of his plant. (If you have a large backyard or garden, you might want to designate a certain section for birthday plants.)

Now pass a bowl of salt water around, so that everyone can wash their hands as a ritual of purification. You may have to hold the bowl for very young children. Allow them to be playful, even splash in the water. This is a joyous occasion. Pass a special towel around to dry hands. Join hands again and recite a blessing: "We thank you God for allowing us to come together to celebrate [name]'s birthday. On this day, [name] promises to honor the earth and to be a responsible member of humankind. To commemorate this new year of her life, she will now give away something of her past."

The birthday person now brings out whatever he has outgrown or a symbol of it—a toy, training wheels from a bicycle, an outgrown or well-used article of clothing, a book from a course he has taken. Even young kids can grasp the idea of releasing something old to make room for new things or new opportunities. At the very least, children as young as two understand what it means to be "bigger"—they might not need a bottle anymore, or a certain stuffed animal, or perhaps they've grown out of a pair of shoes. This is not about sacrificing a treasured object, but merely acknowledging your own growth. An adult or a child who is old enough can spend a moment talking about what giving away the object means to him.

Now give the celebrant an object that represents his next year. A toddler might be given his first tricycle, a teenager his first razor, an adult a briefcase or address book. It can also be a certificate promising to take the child to a restaurant or a sports event, a membership in a gym—any activity that the person wasn't ready to do before this birthday.

Pass around the blank birthday book. Have everyone write something or paste a picture or other bit of memorabilia into the book. Whatever pages aren't used are left for the person to fill in during the year. End the ritual with a traditional birthday cake. Have everyone sing "Happy Birthday" while the celebrant blows out the candles. Hold the balloon over the person's head and allow him to pop it. As the balloon bursts and the candies come pouring out, tell him that this is going to be a year filled with sweetness and joy.

Follow-Up: Each year, review last year's birthday album. Everyone will delight in the memories and be amazed by the person's growth.

RITUAL REALITIES: There are as many variations on birthday celebrations as there are different kinds of families—including fictional ones. In the recent best-seller, *Divine Secrets of the Ya Ya Sisterhood,* the protagonist's mother had a tradition of bringing each birthday child two cakes—one brought into the celebrant's bedroom in the morning, the other reserved for the party later that day. I found many real-life examples as well.

~ I'd known Shelly since she was a little girl, and I can't remember anyone who looked forward to a birthday as much as she did. It was probably because her parents, Don and Joanne, always went all out—a lavish party with entertainment, lots of presents, and as many guests as Shelly wanted to invite. Shelly went away to school when she was fourteen, and her fifteenth birthday fell on a weekday. Joanne called for my advice. Since they couldn't be with Shelly, I suggested that they at least send her a birthday book. Don found a funny cartoon that reminded him of his daughter. Joanne wrote a poem. Shelly's older sister, Jamie, added an eagle feather she had found in Seattle and put it in the book for good luck. Uncle Jake pasted in the ticket stubs of a movie he had attended with Shelly two years earlier—which she had no idea that

he had saved. And his wife, Aunt Mamie, put in a pressed flower and wrote beneath it, "This reminds me of the wonderful walks the two of us took last summer." Everyone also contributed a slew of photographs. "All of this would have been more fun with you," Joanne wrote in the note that accompanied the book, "but here is the next best thing." Admittedly, this wasn't an extravagant birthday gift, but, as Shelly confirmed when I talked with her, it was one of the most memorable.

~ Every year on her children's birthdays, Susan incorporates into her ritual the story of how they were born. No matter how many times they hear the details, they delight in the telling. Likewise, other parents use the occasion to recap the previous year, asking guests to prepare anecdotes. Children love to hear stories about themselves.

~ Circumstances can also change the tone of a celebration. There are times when a person's birthday coincides with or reminds one of a tragic or unhappy event. In my friend Marilyn's case, her father died a few days before her forty-fourth birthday. The following year was very hard for Marilyn, and although her husband and children wanted her to "snap out of it," she insisted on celebrating in her own way. Instead of cake and candles, she cooked a dinner that she knew her father liked, and she lit a memorial candle in his honor. After dinner, she brought out an old family album and talked about her dad, telling stories about him that her children had never heard. There were some laughs that evening and many tears. Marilyn felt healed by the occasion and her children learned new things about her and were able to share memories about their grandfather. Afterward, Marilyn told me, "By honoring his memory, it was also a celebration of my own life, because all that he taught me lives on through me and my children."

e◦ *Gotcha Day*

ACCORDING to a seven-year-old girl interviewed by a *New York Times* reporter, adoption is "when people who love you take care of you and become your parents." Every year, thousands of loving men and women do just that. In 1992, over 127,000 children were adopted, more than thirteen thousand of them from other countries. It is now fairly commonplace for even single parents or same-gender couples to adopt children. And now, thanks to the miracles of modern reproductive medicine, adoptions also take place through surrogacy, in which another woman, inseminated or implanted with an embryo, carries the fetus to full term for the prospective mother.

Because of the increase in adoption and advances in nontraditional methods of conception, much of the secrecy and stigma that once obscured such arrangements are thankfully gone. In fact, an increasing number of families today embrace the concept of "open adoption," whereby the biological mother, semen or egg donor, or surrogate is not only known but, in some cases, invited to be in the child's life. It only makes sense, then, that we create a ritual to honor the day when the new arrival comes home. Even in closed adoptions, where the biological parent is not known, it's important that at least *the fact* of adoption is honored.

Adoption rituals have precedence in ancient cultures. Many tribal societies performed ceremonies to welcome visitors into the tribe. These rites often involved some type of exchange, be it gifts or even blood (as in blood brothers), and other acts that symbolized the forming of new ties. If an Iroquois bride marries out of the tribe, her groom is wrapped in a blanket with her and blessed by whoever performs the marriage ceremony. In this way, the groom is officially "adopted" by the tribe.

Community acceptance is a key element in adoption rituals. Among the Camar in northern

India, for example, members of the clan come together, and the parents of the new child announce, "You are now the son of . . ." Everyone then sprinkles the child with rice for good luck, and the adoptive parents give a ceremonial meal to all those present.

Today's adoption rituals ought to include these sentiments as well. The following ritual, suggested to me by a student of mine, Suzi Gerace, is not quite a birthday, not quite an anniversary. Suzie calls it "Gotcha Day." It is designed to show your adopted child how much you wanted him and that every year you continue to cherish him.

Intention: To honor and celebrate the gift of adoption.
Timing: On the anniversary of the day you brought your child home.
Ingredients: Matches, pink candle (love), frankincense (strengthens connection to the Divine), diffuser, baby pictures or videos (if available) and any other pictures representing the child at a younger age, child's favorite food and music (including whatever music was played at his or her Baby Blessing/Naming ceremony, page 70; if your child was adopted from another culture, it's also important to incorporate appropriate foods and music into her annual Gotcha Day celebration.

Recipe: Invite relatives and friends to participate in this joyous ritual. Sit in a circle. Light a pink candle to symbolize the group's love for the child, and ask everyone to take a few deep breaths to center themselves. Begin by thanking your child for coming into the family. Place the frankincense in the diffuser and, as you light it, explain that throughout the ages this scent has been considered precious and filled with spiritual power (which is why it was one of the three gifts the Magi gave to the baby Jesus). You now give it to your child for the same reasons and as a symbol of how precious his life is.

Now go around the circle and, starting with the parent(s), have everyone talk about how important it is to have this child in the family and in the community. The parents should explain (in age-appropriate terms) why and how much they wanted a child, what they had to go through, and what happened on the day they first saw their child. Be as descriptive as possible about the circumstances—going to a hospital, a home, or a lawyer's office, or perhaps making a trip to another country to pick up the child. Talk about what it felt like to hold him, what you did first when you got home, how strange and wonderful it was to have this new life in the house. This story is part of a family legend. Even if the child has heard it a hundred times before, most children delight in the repetition. Let everyone else have a turn to speak. Encourage people to

97

share their remembrances of the child's growing up. If you had a Baby Blessing/Naming ceremony (page 70), show the video, or bring out a family album.

Be aware that adopted children begin to ask about their origins anywhere between ages three and ten, and these queries may come up on Gotcha Day. For example, as much as adoptive parents continually stress how much they wanted their children, a common question from middle school children is "But why didn't my real mother want me?" The child's age, how much you know about the biological mother, and whether you have decided on a closed or open adoption will determine how you answer. (Think about these questions before your child is old enough to ask them.)

To close the ceremony, ask the child to lie in the center of the circle. With a child under eight, you might want to have everyone step forward and, together, lift her body over their heads, to symbolize their high regard for her. As she is held aloft the parents can recite their own blessing or say something like, "God, we thank you for bringing [child's name] into our family and into our community. She is a gift we cherish. Keep her safe, and give her strength, compassion, and wisdom." With an older child, or a younger one who might be embarrassed or frightened by being held aloft, simply have everyone place a hand somewhere on the child's body while the blessing is being recited. End with a ceremonial buffet of all your child's favorite foods and music.

Follow-Up: If you take photographs or make a videotape of your Gotcha Day celebration, show the pictures or video at next year's event.

RITUAL REALITY: Bob, an American, and Michelle, originally from Switzerland, were in their early forties when they decided that they wanted to have a child. After a long, hard road of applications, arrangements, and disappointments, they were told by a Korean agency that they could pick up their baby at the airport. Michelle remembers gasping as she watched several Korean women descend a stairway, babies in their arms. "I was told mine was the one in the lavender blanket." Bob and Michelle kept their baby girl's Korean name, "Jyung-ok," as a middle name, but called her Madeline ("Maddy," for short). Ever since that day, the family has celebrated what they call "A-Day," inviting friends to share Korean food and music but mostly to recount what these parents consider the happiest day of their married life. Over the years, many of their friends have given

Korean dolls and costumes to Maddy on A-Day. The family has added a Korean flavor to many of their everyday rituals as well.

Although not much is known about Maddy's biological mother, Bob and Michelle have always been open with their daughter about adoption, using the word long before Maddy was old enough to understand it. "She was three when she noticed the physical differences," Michelle recalls, "and by four began to ask what her mother was like." Among other bits of memorabilia in Maddy's growing scrapbook, which is supplemented every A-Day, Michelle pasted a brochure showing Korean dancers. "One of them could be my mother," Maddy, then four, observed.

ℰ Parents' Day

MOST OF US buy cards or go out for dinner to commemorate Mother's Day and Father's Day, but we rarely realize how far back these celebrations date. Like many other holidays that have been commercialized in modern times, both these days have centuries-old antecedents.

As early as 2250 B.C., the Romans celebrated a festival of Hilaria, which occurred in the spring and was dedicated to the Mother goddess. During the Middle Ages, people in remote villages attended the main church in their parish—the "mother" church—for a special service. In England, a day known as "Mothering Sunday" fell on the fourth Sunday of Lent and was a time when working people went home to visit their mothers. And in France, *Fête des Mères* ("Mother's Holiday") occurs the last Sunday in May. The French celebration, which calls for Mom to be the center of attention, is not unlike our Mother's Day, a tradition started in 1908 by a West Virginian daughter, Anna Jarvis, to honor her own and other mothers.

Cultural historians suspect that the precursor of Father's Day was the ancient Roman holiday of Parentalia, a festival in honor of deceased parents, which occurred between the thirteenth and twenty-second of February. During that period, ceremonies were held, according to the poet Ovid, "to appease the souls of your fathers." In our early Father's Day celebrations, white roses were used to remember fathers who died; red roses were given to living fathers. In 1910, Spokane, Washington, was the first city to officially acknowledge Father's Day, after which other cities followed suit.

We already have those days to honor our parents, so you might ask, why bother to invent a "Parents' Day"? I see two reasons. First of all, there's often less of a difference between Mom and Dad nowadays—she works out of the house, too; he's also in the kitchen. So it makes sense to have a day honoring their joint dedication to the family. Moreover, with the changing configurations of families, we must learn to use the word "parent" in the broadest sense. We need a more inclusive holiday that honors not only Mom and Dad but also stepparents, foster parents, even godparents, who play an important role in children's lives. My Parents' Day celebration, which is based on the Old English practice of children hanging "May Baskets" on a friend's door as a sign of love and appreciation, can be done by young or adult children. This is not to say that we need to stop honoring Mother's Day or Father's Day. In fact, this ritual can easily be made part of those traditional celebrations.

Intention: To honor the person or people who contribute to your nurturing and care.
Timing: Once a year, on either Mother's Day or Father's Day, or on a meaningful day of your choice. For example, if it's to honor a stepparent, it could be the anniversary of the day she or he first met the children; if for foster parents, when the children first came to live with them.
Ingredients: Essence of vanilla (joy) or vanilla candle, diffuser, matches, a red rose (love), appreciation box (see below), colored paper, flowers, ribbons, candy, poetry, drawings, and pencils and crayons.

To Make an Appreciation Box: This is another one of those projects that could be handled in a Family Meeting (see page 41). Depending on the age of the children, it could be a shoe box or cigar box, or any kind of container that's made in arts and crafts or shop class. Even the youngest members of the family can help out decorating the appreciation box with markers, ribbons, flowers, beads, or jewels.

Preparation: In the week preceding the actual Parents' Day, make an appreciation box (see above). Inside it, place drawings, home-baked cookies, poems, or any other objects and symbols that show love and appreciation for the parent. Write down things that you love about them ("I love the way you bake me banana bread on my birthday" or "I love the way you smile"). Also include written promises to do something special for that person.

Recipe: On the morning of Parents' Day, the children place the appreciation box outside the parents' door. They are not to leave the room. They are allowed to get the box and then have to get back into bed. When the children see that their parents have retrieved the box, that's their cue to bring breakfast in bed. On the tray, they place the vanilla candle and the red rose. After they deliver the breakfast, they light the candle (young children may need help) and present the parents with the rose. Ideally, breakfast should include maple syrup, honey, or a piece of fruit to represent sweetness. Following breakfast in bed, the children make good on the promises they have included in the appreciation box.

If this ritual is done by older children who might live in a different house from the parent(s), it will, of course, be necessary to make some adaptation. Instead of breakfast in bed, for example, you might want to do this ritual later in the day, and inform your parents that you'll be arriving with surprises and food.

RITUAL REALITY: Wanda, a forty-two-year-old hairdresser whose parents had divorced when she was twelve, had grown very close to her stepmother, Grace, especially after her father died unexpectedly in his late fifties. Because her mother was still alive, Mother's Day usually presented what felt like an unresolvable conflict for Wanda. She always sent Grace flowers and cards, but because her own mother was still smarting from feelings of abandonment, Wanda never got to see her stepmother on Mother's Day.

When I told her about my Parents' Day ritual, Wanda was ecstatic. "What a perfect way for me to honor Grace!" she exclaimed. She had no idea when she first met Grace, but she knew it was in December, because she remembered the scarf Grace gave her as "an early Christmas present." Arbitrarily, then, Wanda chose a Sunday in December to make plans with her stepmother. "I just told her to expect me. I had something I wanted to share with her," Wanda recalls. "I also told her that we'd have lunch but that I'd take care of it."

On Sunday, December 22, 1996, Wanda, took the elevator up to Grace's apartment, put her appreciation box at the door, rang the bell, and scurried around the corner of the hallway. She had decorated a shoe box with bright red contact paper and white stickers on which she wrote "Thanks," "You're the best," "I love you," "You've been there," and other expressions of caring and gratitude. On top of the box was a note for Grace:

Dear Grace,
Don't be alarmed—just follow these directions: After you pick up this box, leave the door unlatched, and go into the living room. Sit on the sofa and begin to look inside. I'll be along shortly.

Love,
Wanda

A few minutes later, Wanda let herself in, carrying a shopping bag full of delicacies from Grace's favorite Chinese restaurant. Sweet, joyful tears were rolling down her stepmother's cheeks, especially when she saw Wanda's promise: "From this day forward, you and I will always celebrate December 22 as Stepmother's Day." And they have. Each year, Wanda tells me, she looks forward to decorating the appreciation box in a new way and picking a different food for them to share.

Family Reunion

ONCE UPON A TIME, long ago, families lived from generation to generation in the same village. As children grew up, aunts, uncles, and grandparents played important roles in children's lives. There was an instant hotline, and what happened to family members, from birth to death—their firsts, their accomplishments and their defeats, their illnesses— was common knowledge. Histories were easily passed down from mother to daughter, from father to son.

Today, few children really know or spend time with their grandparents, aunts, uncles, and cousins and rarely on a day-to-day basis. We are lucky if we live near our kin, let alone know what's going on in their lives. And many of us don't make the effort to span the miles. Consequently, we are raising a generation of children who know next to nothing about their family lineage.

Earlier cultures understood how important it is to nurture seeds of the future by anchoring them to roots of the past. For example, many indigenous people, such as those living in the areas from British Columbia to southern Alaska, held annual potlatches, a traditional celebration that was created to honor the connections between a family and its ancestors, as well as to display the wealth of the tribe. People often traveled great distances to attend these events, because everyone recognized that it was important to maintain communication. Guests were invited to share stories of clans and their ancestors as well as to share sacred and secular resources of the tribe. The festivities included dancing, singing, and a distribution of whatever goods were brought to share.

My Family Reunion ritual borrows from the potlatch tradition. Like the ancients, we might have to travel to keep strong ties to our families. Regardless of the sacrifices, we need to make the effort and create times where all members can come together to catch up on each other's lives. This ritual also stresses the importance of honoring older adults, which is particularly important for children. Too often, children are reluctant to talk to older people; they assume they have nothing in common. In other cultures, though, grandparents spend the first two or three years with their grandchildren because it is believed that, in karmic terms, they have the most in common, the child having just evolved from Spirit and the grandparent preparing to return. In our fast-paced lives, a family reunion is a rudder in choppy seas. It helps both adults and children feel centered, secure, and known.

Intention: To share family history and create new memories, and to honor one's living elders.
Timing: Once a year; more often, if family members can manage it.
Ingredients: Low table, salt (purification), parsley (protection), matches, white candle (remembrance), family medicine bundle (see below), leather thong or ribbon, photographs and other family mementos, essence of rosemary (strong bond), diffuser, talking stick (page 42), favorite foods, wine or juice, something to give away. One family member should be in charge of videotaping or recording this ritual.

Making a Family Medicine Bundle:
The oldest female of your "tribe," such as a grandmother or a great-aunt, should be asked to present a medicine bundle to the family. She should select a special cloth—an heirloom napkin or a piece of fabric—that reminds her of the old country. Even if your family has been here for several generations, we all date back to some other country, or at least some long-forgotten tradition, as is the case with those of Native American descent. She should also choose a symbol that is sacred to her, such as a crucifix, a statue of a god or goddess, a locket or other piece of jewelry that belonged to one of her grandparents. At the ceremony, the object will be wrapped in the sacred cloth.

Recipe: Send invitations to several generations of family members; include nonrelatives who are close to the family. Explain the ritual in advance and ask them to bring their favorite family photos to the reunion or an item of value that they wish to contribute to a family altar.

On the day of the reunion, after everyone has arrived, family members form a circle around the low table. The Elder walks around the outside of the circle, sprinkling salt to purify the space and to sanctify the gathering. She gives each person a piece of parsley to eat for protection.

Light the white candle for those who are no longer with you. This may bring up tears, so don't rush this part. Be sensitive and allow time for people to express these emotions, silently or by saying that they miss the person.

The next phase of the ritual involves creating a family altar. The Elder will bring out the contents of her medicine bundle and explain why she has chosen the cloth. She places the sacred object in it and shares its significance. The oldest male present now wraps the medicine bundle with a leather thong or ribbon. This is the first item placed on the family altar. Other guests then add pictures or any special keepsakes that remind them of your family history—a silver cup handed down from a great-grandparent, a household item, letters, medals, trophies. Small children should participate, too, by making something or contributing a small toy. Finally, the participants should place around the altar the items they've brought to give away.

As the sharing portion of the ritual is about to begin, explain that you are placing a few drops of essence of rosemary into the diffuser to stimulate memory. Using the talking stick, go around the circle and give people a chance to share personal remembrances. Even young children can talk about their earliest memories. Also, ask the elders about their or your childhood. Many of our ancestors came from other countries, and we have lost their stories. This is a perfect time to reclaim your family history. You may ask your grandmother what her life was like when she was a teenager. Your uncle may remember playing with you and your sister when you were children. Your cousin may talk about memories of your tenth birthday.

Imagine that you are weaving a tapestry of family history, with each person's story adding a thread. This not only strengthens family ties, but also allows new members—spouses, stepparents, in-laws, and friends—to hear and become an integral part of the history of the family that they have joined. It gives children a sense of security to feel connected and to see how they are like their ancestors. Knowing that a great-uncle was an artist or that a grandfather loved opera can both explain and validate a child's budding interests.

Go around the circle a second time, asking each person to share an important event that happened to them that year. They might share something that they are proud of, something difficult that they managed to overcome, something that they wished they had done differently. Stress that you are not there to judge one another but merely to become acquainted on a deeper level. (Depending on the size of your family, you may want to put a time limit on sharing.) Everyone gets to pick something from the offering pile, being careful not to take what he or she brought but rather to accept a gift from another family member. End with a toast of wine or juice and a family picnic.

RITUAL REALITY:

In 1994, my father was diagnosed with lung cancer. During the six-month period of my father's illness, I spent as much time as possible with him, asking him to tell stories about his childhood, about my grandparents, and relatives that I had never met. I wanted to interview him on video, but at the time he was too ill. I felt compelled to find out every detail of his life; it was almost as if this would keep him with me. Only after he died did I find a way to really make that happen.

My brother Mark has always been our family historian, and the first year after our father died, Mark decided to have a family reunion at his home in Vermont. The guests ranged in age from six to ninety-two, and represented four generations of our family, as well as friends of my parents who had stayed in touch. I knew little about my maternal grandparents, so I asked my mother to talk about her parents and grandparents. My

father's brother's friend told me what my father was like as a boy. As dozens of stories were shared around the kitchen table, we were often moved to tears and laughter. I delighted in spending time with aunts, uncles, and cousins whom I hardly ever see, really getting to know them. Afterward, we sang songs around a bonfire.

Although we didn't plan it this way initially, a reunion at Mark's house has become an annual family ritual, and each year the gathering grows, to include more distant relatives and close friends. One year, when Mark didn't feel up to the task of hosting the event, he canceled—well, he *tried* to cancel. People were so upset, they showed up anyway, many of them camping out. He was so moved by everyone's drive to reunite, Mark hosted our gathering after all.

Every year, I've captured our stories on videotape, and now, as part of the ritual, we watch last year's tape. Not only is it heartwarming, sad, and funny to review, but also it's a living testament to each family member's growth. For instance, my fifteen-year-old nephew, Joel, who was once too shy to speak on camera, now could speak for hours ... if we let him! I'm struck, too, by the irony of our using modern technology in this way. Before television, people entertained themselves by gathering together to hear the elders of the community recite the history of the clan. Our ritual is a link between the past and the future, and our videotapes a sacred family treasure.

7. Seasonal Celebrations

EVERY FAMILY CELEBRATES holidays that have seasonal overtones. Christmas, Hanakkah, and Kwanza inevitably evoke thoughts of a winter wonderland, while Memorial Day and the Fourth of July mark the happy times of summer. Who could imagine Halloween or Thanksgiving occurring at any time but autumn? Likewise, Easter and Passover with their themes of rebirth conjure the spirit of spring.

Unfortunately, when most of us commemorate such special days, we rarely think about, and in some cases don't even know, that many holidays—"holy days"—were originally created to mark the changing of seasons and other happenings in nature. Even worse, as our celebrations have become less about meaning and more about material concerns—getting presents or wearing new outfits—holidays can be both stressful and laden with unrealistic expectations. Reflecting this phenomenon is one of the funnier *Seinfeld* TV episodes in which Jerry's friend George

recalls that his father resented the commercialization of Christmas. He fought back by inventing his own tradition, "Festivus . . . for the rest of us." In lieu of a tree, Mr. Costanza brought home an aluminum pole!

The "rest of us" need not be quite so subversive to restore meaning to our holiday traditions. We can look to our ancestors, who planned their rituals to coincide with the changes in the seasons. They believed there was a direct relationship to the elements, the stars, and to Spirit/God, who directs all things. Because they needed a way to predict and honor the seasons, they routinely celebrated moon cycles, the solstices (when the sun is at its greatest distance from the celestial equator and appears to stand still), and the equinoxes (when the sun crosses the plane of the earth's equator, making night and day of equal length all over the earth). Many native people still live by these markers.

However, we in the so-called civilized world

barely notice the seasons, especially if we live in large cities or in perpetually temperate climates. Were it not for a change of weather and the different clothing required, we would have no sense of the cycles of the sun and moon. In the name of progress, we unwittingly have separated ourselves from nature. Thanks to technology, snowplows immediately clear the streets of snow, and air conditioners take the heat out of summer. Furthermore, most of us don't grow our own food crops; we opt for convenience, buying summer fruit in the middle of winter, winter squash in May, drinking milk that comes from cartons not cows. When nature really nudges us to pay attention, as on an extremely hot and humid day or when it's bitter cold outside, we may comment about the weather, or complain. But we rarely think about the significance of the season— whether plants are lying dormant or growing, whether animals are resting or bearing their young. In short, we have lost our intimate connection with the earth. Until recently, we hadn't even given much thought or energy to the precious resources we've wasted. (Earth Day only dates back to 1970!)

The truth is, we need more than the observance of a *day* to regain a sense of connection to nature and to remind ourselves to respect our planet and the life it sustains. The suggestions in this chapter will help you do just that. I offer a special ritual for each of the four yearly transitions, each done at its corresponding time of day: winter (midnight), spring (dawn), summer (noon), and autumn (dusk). Here I have included a chart of the elements, directions, and symbols most commonly associated with each of the seasons, should you choose to incorporate this information into the seasonal rituals you create.

Season	Element	Time of Day	Direction	Scents	Colors	Animals	Objects
SPRING	air	dawn	east	basil, bergamot, mint, dill, parsley	yellow, white	eagle	feathers, wind chimes
SUMMER	fire	noon	south	frankincense, copal, black pepper, clove, lime, rosemary, ginger	red, orange	coyote, mouse	candles, bonfires, hot peppers
AUTUMN	water	dusk	west	sandalwood, chamomile, freesia, iris, jasmine, rose, vanilla, ylang-ylang	blue, green, turquoise, indigo	bear, raven	glass, cup, bowl, ocean, river, lake, stream, juice, wine
WINTER	earth	midnight	north	pine, cedar, vetivert, spicknard, honeysuckle, lilac	brown, green	buffalo, white owl	plants, flowers, dirt, salt, grains, bread

If you already celebrate several seasonal holidays in your family, you might want to incorporate parts of these rituals into your own traditions. Or, you might make up your own all-purpose tradition, as one couple did when they created Seasonfest (see Ritual Realities, pages 127–129). The important point is to honor these seasonal transitions—to experience them and think about their significance, not just read them on a calendar. In this way, the passage of time and the movement of the planets become concrete and meaningful to you and your children, and you will all feel more connected to the cycles of nature and to Mother Earth.

❧ Winter

WINTER is a quiet time of rest and renewal, a time when nature goes underground. The winter solstice is the shortest day of the year and the longest night. Out of the darkness of winter comes the promise of spring. It is on the winter solstice that many cultures believe that the archetypal Great Mother gave birth to a sun child—the Egyptian deity Isis gave birth to Horus, the sun god; the Greek Leto gave birth to a shining Apollo. In the matriarchal religions, the rebirth of the goddess herself was celebrated—Persephone (Greek), Besana (Italian), Sunne (Scandinavian), and Sun Woman (Australian).

Although not all geographic locales are necessarily cold in December, winter is universally synonymous with darkness. Many myths deal with the disappearance of light and a return or calling back of the sun. One such tale, according to Donna Henes, author of *Celestial Auspicious Occasions,* can be found in Japanese mythology.

Amaterasu, the sun goddess, hid in a cave to escape the taunts of her brother Sus-wono. In her absence, the world is suddenly plunged into darkness. However, on the winter solstice, Alarming Woman, a sacred clown, succeeds in enticing her out, thereby restoring light to the world.

Not surprisingly, many cultures celebrate festivals of light during the winter months. Chanukah, the Jewish holiday that occurs in December, commemorates a time when the Temple of Jerusalem was under siege and a tiny bit of oil miraculously burned for eight days; today, a candle is lit to remember each of those eight nights. In Sweden, on December 13, Santa Lucia Day, which honors the patron saint of light, young girls wear crowns made of candles and lingonberries. Hindus also celebrate a festival of lights, Diwali. Along all the pathways in a town or village, the celebrants light *diye,* small clay lanterns filled with oil and a burning cotton wick, to welcome the god Rama, the Hindu god of fertility, and to honor Lakshmi, the goddess of prosperity.

In many countries, candles also play a major role in the rites of Christmas, a word derived from the Old English *Chistes masse,* meaning "mass of Christ." Known as *Navidad* in Latin countries, *Noël* in France, and *Natale* in Italy, the holiday commemorates the birth of Jesus and, in most countries, is celebrated on December 25, although the actual date of Jesus' birth is unknown. Kwanza, an African American winter holiday that has been celebrated since 1966, also involves candles; seven are lit, representing the seven African Principles.

The winter ritual that follows draws from many of the above traditions and can be done alone or incorporated into rites you already observe.

Intention: To honor the winter season.
Timing: An evening (after the sun has set) around the winter solstice (December 20–23).
Ingredients: Evergreen branch (new life), cedar branch (spirituality), pine needles (healing, purification), rosemary (love), frankincense (spirituality), crushed cinnamon sticks (happiness and prosperity), animal totems chosen by the participants (pages 20–21), barrel or large flowerpot filled with sand, one yellow candle for each member of the family (solar principle) plus two extra candles, matches, store-bought or homemade percussion instruments (see below), a red envelope filled with make-believe money, homemade gift for each person (painted rocks, cards, cookies, decorated boxes).

Making Percussion Instruments: To get ready for this ritual, even young children can make percussion instruments (page 18).

Recipe: In preparation, set up a small area within a room to achieve the feeling of a cave— drapes drawn, a canopy (or sheet overhead), pillows to mark the location of "walls." In the center of the area, set up an altar with the evergreen and cedar branches, pine needles, rosemary, frankincense, and crushed cinnamon sticks. Using the Animal Medicine Cards (page 20), drawings, or pictures cut out of magazines, members of the family and friends who participate should pick an animal totem to guide them through the winter, and place these on the altar as well. Finally, position the barrel filled with sand near the altar and lay the yellow candles around its base.

Have everyone sit in a circle and then turn off all the lights except for a small lamp or night-light in another area of the room, so that your "cave" is lit only by the dim, indirect light. Everyone should have a percussion instrument handy. Take a moment to feel the darkness of winter and to breathe in the aroma of the pine, cedar, rosemary, and cinnamon. Light the frankincense. This is a good time to tell stories from mythology about the return of the sun. Tell a tale your grandparents told or find good stories in the library. Here's one that Native Americans in the Pacific Northwest tell about Raven, who saved the sun from a selfish old chief who refused to share it:

When the world became dark, Raven turned himself into a pine needle and floated down the river, where he was swallowed by the chief's daughter, who was at that very moment taking a cool drink of water. She became pregnant and gave birth to a son who was Raven in disguise. The only way the baby would stop crying was when the chief gave him a ball of light to play with. Raven then flew upward and installed the ball of light in the sky so that everyone else in the tribe could have light and warmth, too.

Share your ideas about winter, what you love about it, what you dislike. Children might be excited about the snow and the fact that they soon can ski and go sledding, but they hate all the extra clothes they have to wear. Adults might look forward to the quiet of winter but not the slushy roads. After everyone discusses what they like and don't like about the season, they should explain why they chose their animal totems. Jody says her hummingbird reminds her to lighten up when things feel heavy. To Steven, the bear gives him permission to take time to retreat and regroup when his life is too busy.

Now "call back" the sun with music. Have one person start the rhythmic beat and others follow suit with their instruments. You can also hum. Keep this up for five minutes—the children will love it. Then, one by one, each person places a candle in the barrel filled with sand, lights it, and makes a wish for the coming season. When everyone has finished, light the two additional candles, one for the earth and one for the sun. The room will soon become infused with your collective light, a symbol that you have brought in the sun.

Pass the red envelope filled with play money around the circle to allow everyone to touch it, and have the last person burn the envelope in the fireplace or in a fireproof bowl, to manifest good fortune for everyone in the coming year.

The last step is to come up with a family project to help the earth. You might decide to plant a tree, help a homeless family, use less electricity, recycle, or take homemade cookies to a nursing home. Finally, share your gifts and winter treats.

Follow–Up: As a family, experience different winter customs this year. Research another country's or a different religion's holiday celebration. If you've never done it before, attend a Kwanza party, celebrate Chanukah, go to Midnight Mass. Or, you might go to an ethnic fair or a festival associated with the winter solstice.

RITUAL REALITY: Although both Paul and Leanne were natives of Minnesota, they first met and fell in love in Hawaii. He was at a Waikiki naval base and, coincidentally, she was on winter holiday. They also fell in love with the climate, so after they married, they set up their new home on Oahu and, eventually, started a family. Rituals were very important to both of them; they not only celebrated Christmas annually but also the winter solstice. They put Christmas lights on palm trees, and welcomed winter surrounded by flowers and leis. However, they recognized that their children couldn't really grasp the true meaning of winter—at least, not as Paul and Leanne had experienced it as kids. They decided that it was time for their children to see snow.

Getting ready for a Minnesota winter was no small project, because it meant outfitting the children right down to snowsuits and boots. The excitement began to build weeks before the trip and reached a fever pitch as the plane began to descend over the state. In place of the lush tropical paradise they were used to, the children saw below them miles of white punctuated by dark green pine trees—a sight they had seen only in books.

Grandma and Grandpa (with Paul's and Leanne's prompting) had prepared their yard for a special winter welcoming ceremony. They had placed a circle of large candles in the snow, and (once the children had changed into their new winter clothes) they invited them into the circle. They made a large bonfire, sat on wooden stools around it, and told stories of what it had been like for their parents, who had lived in Sweden before emigrating to Minnesota. Of course, what the children loved most was frolicking in the four-foot-high snowdrifts and building their first snowman. Afterward, the family said a prayer to thank God for the experience. They concluded the ritual with hot cocoa, mulled cider, and Grandma's special sun cookies.

Spring

SPRING marks a resurrection from winter. It is a time of rebirth and revival, full of new possibilities. In Greek mythology, it was the time when Persephone returned from the underworld, and everything bloomed again. April 1, in fact, used to be considered New Year's Day, and anyone who didn't realize this was considered an "April fool." Most of us love to celebrate this season. We observe Arbor Day by planting trees, and on Earth Day we clean up our parks, riverbanks, and wilderness areas. We take trips to see the tulips or cherry blossoms in bloom. We're not alone in that spring tradition: In Japan, millions of people flock to their parks for "Hanami," their cherry blossom festival. And all over the world major religious events are celebrated in spring. Easter, named for the ancient Saxon goddess *Eostre,* commemorates the resurrection of Christ. Passover marks the Jewish people's flight to freedom from Egypt, where they had been enslaved.

Almost every culture, past and present, has some sort of ritual to celebrate the promise and fertility of spring. In ancient Rome, the lengthening of the day that followed the vernal (spring) equinox was marked by sacrifices to celebrate the death and rebirth of Attis, the god of vegetation. Various goddesses of fertility—the Greeks' Aphrodite, the Native American Spider Woman, Mexico's Tonantzin, the African goddess Oshun, the Norwegians' Freya, and the Roman goddess Flora—were all honored in the spring. May Day is still celebrated in England, where they decorate with flowers, play music, and dance around a "Maypole" adorned with brightly colored ribbons. Every year, some lucky girl is crowned Queen of the May. May is also considered the month of the Virgin Mary.

Not surprisingly, the egg—the universal symbol of rebirth—finds its way into many different types of spring rituals. In ancient Persia, Greece, Egypt, and Rome, red eggs, representing life and rebirth, were given as gifts during the spring. In our modern-day celebrations of Easter, children all over the world still decorate eggs. Every year, an annual Easter egg hunt is held on the lawn of the White House. At Passover Seders, guests dip eggs in salt water as a reminder of the sacrifices made in the ancient temples. In the Greek Orthodox Church, everyone is given a red egg on Easter, representing the rebirth of Christ. Afterward, as people sit around the dinner table, everyone taps eggs with his or her neighbor, the way one would clink glasses when making a toast. If your egg does not crack, it's considered good luck for the coming year.

It was once thought that if you bathed your face in the early morning dew of spring, you would have beauty all year long. When we think of spring nowadays, we imagine taking off the heavy clothes of winter, seeing buds burst with new life, and children being able to play outside later as the days begin to lengthen. We might be motivated to clean the house, or to start a new project that's been germinating over the winter. In any case, most of us gleefully welcome this season. This ritual can help you get spring off to a good start.

Intention: To honor the rebirth of spring.

Timing: The morning of the first sunny day around the time of the vernal equinox (March 21–23).

Ingredients: Matches, lilac incense (to refresh), daffodils (new beginnings), violets (regeneration), amber (balance), topaz (new beginnings), grains such as oats, barley, or rice (nourishment), seeds to plant, a Maypole (see below), a picnic box or basket containing foods that represent spring, such as hard-boiled eggs, sprouts, edible flowers, parsley, and fruits and vegetables of the season, items to donate.

Making a Maypole: The "pole" part can be a small, slender tree, or any kind of pole, approximately six feet in length and one or two inches in diameter (laundry pole, broomstick). Dig a hole for the pole at least one foot deep and wedge the base with rocks. The colored ribbons should be cut to lengths about one and a half times as long as the pole and, at the time of the ritual, tied to the top.

Recipe: This ceremony is best if done outdoors, so your first order of business is to find a place in nature that you and your family can adopt. If you live in a city, go to a park or, if you can, take a day trip out to the country. Ideally, you will find or even borrow a little patch of land that you can observe and commit to taking care of throughout the year. (You might also hold other special family events there.)

The ritual begins at home, with everyone getting up early and pitching in toward a spring cleaning effort. Gather clothes, toys, and other items that family members are ready to donate to a shelter, a school, or a needy family. To reenforce the idea that it is a blessing to give, make sure that adults and children relinquish at least some possessions that they still value, not just things they want to get rid of. When you've finished the spring cleaning, light the incense to refresh and purify your home.

Go to your special place in nature. Create an altar with the daffodils and violets, amber and topaz. Explain the meaning of each to the other participants (see ingredients on pages 14–15, 19). Sit on the earth surrounding the altar. Take a few deep breaths and take in the spring air. Smell it; taste it. Even if it is a cool day, you can feel the potential of the new season in the air. Take a moment of silence—this is a time to honor the planet. Feel the ground underneath you and the sun shining down onto the earth, and imagine its warmth bringing growth and abundance to all humankind. Ask everyone to look around for signs of spring, and play the "I

see" game: "I see little buds on that tree," "I see a robin." Children love to play and it makes them more aware of spring and more observant in general. Have one of the children recite or make up a prayer to the earth. (You might look at the ones offered in *Earth Prayers from Around the World* by Elizabeth Roberts and Elias Amidon; see Sources, page 173.)

Now offer up the grains you have brought to thank the earth for sustaining you through the winter. Each person then plants seeds for the coming year, explaining their purpose. For example, "I plant this seed for happiness," "I plant this seed for friendship," "I plant this seed for patience." When everyone has finished, say, "May all the seeds that we have planted multiply a thousand-fold and may our wishes bring goodness to all concerned." Each of you will be responsible for nurturing your seedling through the coming season.

Now is the time for singing and dancing. Erect the Maypole and attach the colored ribbons. Some dance clockwise and some counterclockwise, alternating under and over one another. As you dance around the Maypole in this pattern, your movements will weave the ribbons into a quilt of color that will make your dreams come true. End by having a picnic of the spring foods you have chosen.

If you are unable to do this ritual outside, it is possible to set up a Maypole indoors, using a Christmas tree stand. In any case, you can easily do the most important part of it—the planting—indoors. Set up your altar in a sunny part of the house. Plant seeds in potting soil, or grow sprouts by putting seeds in a glass jar filled with water. Let the seeds soak overnight; rinse and drain them twice a day until they begin to germinate. When the sprouts appear, place in the sun until they turn green and are ready to eat.

Follow-Up: As a family, experience a different spring custom this year. Research another country's or a different religion's holiday celebration. If you're Christian, attend a Passover Seder, if Jewish, paint Easter eggs or attend an Easter service. Partake in Earth Day celebrations or attend some other type of spring fair or festival.

RITUAL REALITY: Wan-li, a Taiwanese-American, and Deborah, a Sephardic Jew, began to celebrate spring out of desperation. The partners, both in their early forties, met at a Buddhist workshop and, after a whirlwind courtship, tied the marital knot. They came to me shortly before their first anniversary, by which time Deborah, who had always wanted children, was in her eighth month.

"We need a King Solomon," she explained, "because both our families are tearing us apart.

Wan-li's parents converted to Christianity when they came here, and Easter is very important to them. My parents, of course, celebrate Passover. If we choose one over the other, we're bound to insult someone." Wan-li added that although the two of them were weathering the holiday storms, they were worried about the future. "I don't want our child to be born into this kind of tension. And if our parents are this possessive now, imagine how they'll fight over grandchildren."

I suggested dodging the issue by inviting their two families to a spring celebration—parents, grandparents, aunts, uncles, and cousins. Both sets of parents were appalled at such a "New Agey" idea. They never understood why their children were flirting with Buddhism in the first place. And now, with this latest undertaking, they feared that Wan-li and Deborah were abandoning religion all together. However, Wan-li and Deborah convinced everyone to at least attend and then draw their own conclusions. All they asked of each guest was a spring food, preferably items with strong ethnic overtones.

Luckily, Wan-li and Deborah's house had a huge, magnificent backyard, bursting with the promise of spring. They did the above ritual (without the Maypole), but in addition, they included elements of their childhood celebrations on the altar. To honor his Taiwanese heritage, Wan-li added *lin guo* (a sticky rice cake) and a red dragon, symbolizing long life and prosperity. To pay homage to her ancient ties, Deborah added *charoset* (a mixture of chopped apples, walnuts, wine, and cinnamon), which at the Passover Seder represents the mortar Jews were forced to make when they were enslaved in Egypt, and her great-grandfather's yarmulke. And, of course, they also included objects that represented their shared commitment to Buddhism: prayer beads, a statue of Buddha, and incense that was blessed by the Dalai Lama. They explained each of the items on the altar to their guests, stressing that they weren't abandoning their roots, they were strengthening them and making them grow into new life.

Even the oldest members of the family delighted in the planting part of the ritual, which was done in what Wan-li and Deborah explained was the "family garden," a plot that they'd add to every year. Afterward, they feasted on the offerings everyone had brought. Not only did this ritual help solve the couple's dilemma, but bringing their families together stressed what they all had in common—concern for their children, faith (regardless of how it was observed), and a love of good food. After much laughter and music-making, the day ended with a commitment to celebrate spring next year . . . with their grandchild.

❧ Summer

SUMMER is a time of celebration, of prosperity and abundance. How eagerly we all look forward to our summer vacations. With its long days and short nights, summer is synonymous with love and romance. It's no wonder that June is still the most popular bridal month. Interestingly, this harkens back to the ancient times, when ceremonies were performed to represent symbolic marriages between mortals and gods.

Traditionally, cultures around the world have seen summer as a celebration of the strength and fertility of Mother Earth and of other goddesses who represent the Divine Feminine. The Romans dedicated the summer solstice to Vesta, goddess of the hearth, and the Greeks to Hestia, who served the same purpose in their culture. Because this is a time when the sun begins to wane (it waxes after the winter solstice), ancient cultures in Denmark, Norway, Austria, Germany, Britain, and Spain, as well as native people in North Africa and South America, lit bonfires to guarantee the sun's return next year. Often, as part of these rituals, celebrants picked prized summer flowers and herbs—mugwort, chamomile, geranium, St.-John's-wort, thyme, and pennyroyal—to throw on their festival bonfires. They believed these fires would banish sickness from their livestock and their families. For good luck, they jumped across the fire and even walked on hot coals, a precursor to the fire-walking ceremonies practiced today.

Traveling around the globe nowadays one can find other summer rituals that echo these ancient beliefs. In Swaziland, the most important festival of the year, Incwala, which honors kinship, is always held on the summer solstice. Part of the ceremony involves a burning of ceremonial objects that represent the death of the king—the sun—followed by purification and a ceremonial rebirth. The Swahilis believe that this practice ensures good leadership and a prosperous year.

Here in America, we tend to define the beginning, middle, and end of summer by our civil holidays—Memorial Day, July Fourth, and Labor Day. However, the following ritual will remind us of the real marker of summer, the sun.

Intention: To celebrate summer and the power of the sun.

Timing: At noon around the time of the summer solstice (June 21–23).

Ingredients: Yellow (power) and orange (playfulness) candles, matches, copal incense or resin (purification), fireproof bowl, ginger (love), summer flowers of your region, paper plates, carnelian (power and creativity), bloodstone (courage and renewal) or other colored stones of red, orange, gold (colors of the sun), paint, markers, glue, sunflower seeds (good luck), spool of red thread.

Recipe: This ritual is best done outdoors on a very sunny day. Prepare an altar with the candles, matches, incense, essence of ginger, and summer flowers, which represent the lush growth and beauty of the season. You can also add symbols of the sun, such as sunflowers, or a spiritual figure, such as the Egyptian sun god Osiris or the Hawaiian fire goddess Pele, as well as personal mementos that remind you of the summer, like suntan lotion, a shell, a souvenir from camp or a previous summer vacation, a piece of summer fruit.

Begin the ritual as close to noon as possible. To create a sacred space, sit in a circle and light the copal in a fireproof bowl. Take a deep breath and feel the heat of the sun bathing your body. As you light the yellow candle, say a prayer honoring the power of the sun: "Thank you, God, for giving us sun, which keeps us warm, gives us light, and nurtures everything living."

Each person takes a paper plate and, using colored stones and paint, makes a sun power disk—a protective symbol honoring the power of the sun. Draw symbols that can help you have courage, power, passion. Use the colored stones to represent the qualities you want or need. Add the sunflower seeds for good luck. If you want, include a picture of your power animal on the sun disk. These can be hung up near your bed to protect you all year.

Now carefully place a few drops of the ginger essence on the orange candle, light it, and place the burning candle in the center of your circle. Each person should jump over it three times to bring in good fortune. Be careful with little ones; very young children can be picked up and carried over.

Finally, each person takes a length of red thread (approximately twelve inches) and ties five to seven knots in it. Make a wish with each knot. Help each other tie the string around your wrists to bring you summer love—or to strengthen the love you already have. Wear it until it eventually falls off or wears out.

End the ritual with a summer barbecue or picnic.

Follow-Up: Take this opportunity to teach children the *why* of seasons. During the summer, keep track of the sun's path. Young children especially delight in discovering that as the earth moves in its rotation around the sun, the sun appears to be moving, rising in different places and getting continually lower in the sky and at more of an angle as summer wears on. You can track this by keeping a summer diary, standing in a particular place at the same time every week, and noting the position of the sun—how high it is and at what angle it shines down. Or, you can make a sun dial, and observe how the shadow changes.

RITUAL REALITY: Marsha, a thirty-nine-year-old single mother in New York, doesn't see her twelve-year-old son, Dirk, during July and August through Labor Day, because he spends that time with his dad, who lives in Florida. So Marsha does what she calls a "summer promises" ritual with him on June 21, which honors the season and makes their separation easier. It begins with the two of them taking a walk in nature. When they find a spot they both like, they spend a stretch of time (usually around a half hour but no one times it) in silence together, looking around them, lying in the new summer grass, feeling the warmth of the sun. After this quiet meditation, they talk about what summer means to each of them, what they like and dislike about it, what they do, what they'd like to do. Then they make lists of summer promises—to themselves, to each other, and to others. At the end of the hour, they read their lists aloud. Finally, they come up with one last promise: something they'll do together when Dirk gets back.

One year, for example, Dirk promised Marsha he'd call and write more, not only to her but to his grandparents (her parents); he also promised himself he'd try to get along better with his new stepmother and stepsister. Marsha promised him she wouldn't cry when she put him on the plane (which, he had told her, embarrassed him); she promised herself she'd take that class in pottery she'd been talking about. When he got back from visiting his dad that year, Mother and son went out to dinner (as they had promised each other) to Dirk's favorite restaurant, where they reviewed their lists to see how many promises they were able to keep.

Autumn

IN ALMOST every corner of the world, autumn is a time of harvest, reflection, and reverence for our ancestors, and many fall holidays reveal those very themes. In Melanesia, people make rice dollies (dolls) out of the last plants of the harvest; in England, they make corn dollies. Both practices represent the belief that the spirit of the grain will stay alive, thereby ensuring another good harvest. In Germany, Oktoberfest celebrates the hops harvest. The Chinese celebrate the Harvest Moon Festival by eating special moon cakes and catching the moon's reflection in a bowl of water. A similar holiday is observed in Vietnam—the mid-fall festival of Trung Thu—which celebrates the beauty of the moon by eating moon cakes, lighting incense, and making special star lanterns.

Fall is also a time for honoring the connection between the living and the dead, as well as the natural order of life, death, and regeneration. It's no accident that after the Jewish New Year, Rosh Hashana, comes Yom Kippur, the day of atonement and also a time when the deceased are honored, and then Sukkot, the harvest festival. Samhain, the Celtic New Year, which falls on October 31, is a day in which it is believed we can more easily communicate with our ancestors. Similar rituals include the Mexican Day of the Dead on November 2, and the Christian All Souls' Day. During the Trung Thu holiday, in fact, the Vietnamese burn fake money as a way of ensuring good luck for the departed.

Whether we're aware of their deeper significance or not, even our most simple and commonplace autumn traditions, such as apple picking and dressing up for Halloween, reflect these themes. Halloween, the eve of All Saints' Day, was originally conceived as a holiday to honor the dead. In fact, it's called *Día de Los Muertos* in the Latin culture, where people celebrate by going to the cemetery and having picnics with the spirits of the departed.

This fall ritual will help make you conscious of the true meaning of autumn, encouraging families to appreciate what they reap in life, to look toward the future, and to honor their ancestors.

Intention: To celebrate autumn, recognize personal progress, and honor one's ancestors.
Timing: At dusk around the time of the autumn equinox (September 21–23).
Ingredients: Fall flowers, gourds, and fruits, homemade dishes reminiscent of autumn, matches, charcoal, charocoal lighter, vetivert (protection) or patchouli (energy, money), green, yellow, orange, red, and brown candles (the autumn transition), talking stick (page 42), an apple or apples, cut up into as many pieces as there are participants, essence of vanilla (joy), orange (happiness), tiny bowl, and ancestors' house (see below). *Optional:* gourds and beans.

Making an Ancestors' House: The purpose of this small house is to honor your ancestors. The basic structure, which needn't be taller than a foot high, can be made by using spare wood and nails in your workshop, by gluing together cardboard from cartons, by adapting a store-bought dollhouse, or by simply converting a shoe box or large cereal carton into a house. The important thing is that this is an object you all create together, everyone decorating the house with personal symbols that remind them of your ancestors. It could be a picture of your grandfather's motorcycle, a flower your grandmother loved. You can also paste portraits of your ancestors on the inside of the house.

Recipe: Invite family and friends to share this ritual and a potluck harvest feast afterward. Ask them to bring foods of the season—homemade, if possible. On the day of the ritual, decorate the room with fall flowers, gourds, fruits, and other items that evoke the feeling of autumn. As your guests arrive, set out a spread of the fall foods, with the exception of the cut-up apple(s), which should be near the person conducting the ritual. Make an altar of the remaining ingredients above, including the ancestors' house.

Begin by having everyone sit in a circle surrounding the altar. Take a few deep breaths to center yourselves. Light the charcoal and place a few drops of vetivert or patchouli on the burning embers. Now light the candles, first the green, then the yellow, orange, red, and finally the brown, explaining that this symbolizes the transition of the earth, going from the greens of summer to the magnificent colors of fall.

Pass around the talking stick and give each person a chance to share what he or she has personally "harvested" this season. This is a time for acknowledging one's own and one another's accomplishments, no matter how small. Of course, include the little ones. You may have to help them participate by reminding them of their accomplishments—eating or dressing by themselves, starting a new school, joining the choir. Pass around the cut-up apple, and have everyone take a piece to signify acceptance of the abundance and health they've been given.

Place a few drops of vanilla in a tiny bowl and pass it around too, allowing everyone to inhale the essence and become infused with joy. Then place the bowl inside your ancestors' house to ensure the happiness of those who have passed on. Allow people to reminisce about relatives who have died. Even if the younger children never knew Grandpa or Auntie, it's important to share stories about them. Someone might recall Grandma's fall apple pies, for example, or the great pumpkins that Uncle Bob once carved.

Hold hands and say a prayer of thanks together, something you have written for the occasion (and made copies of for everyone to read), or a simple blessing, such as "Dear God, we thank you for the bounty of this season."

If you live in a house, leave your ancestors' house in front of the front door for protection; or, if you live in an apartment, on your family altar.

Now enjoy the benefits of the season by eating the food that everyone has contributed.

Optional: Cut a small opening in a gourd, and fill with dried beans. Glue the opening closed, and you have a rattle. Make one for each person. Now sing, dance, and celebrate!

RITUAL REALITIES: Moving from one geographic locale to another often alters the way you view and celebrate the changing seasons. In some instances, families become more aware; in others, even noticing the seasons is difficult, because the physical signs are absent or different. The two ritual realities below are instances in which families who moved came up with creative ways to acknowledge the seasons:

When her mother's sight began failing, Patty, a twenty-nine-year-old teacher, decided to move from Vermont to her native Arizona, where her mother still lived. Patty had stayed in Burlington after college, but she never really got used to the cold weather. Besides, she knew it would be easy to find a teaching job in Tucson. Her older sister lived there with her four children, and Patty looked forward to getting to know her nieces and nephews, as well as other extended family members whom she had left behind.

"After a year in Arizona," Patty wrote me, "the only thing I miss—besides some of my good friends in Vermont—is the change of seasons, especially fall." I suggested that Patty get her whole family involved in doing the fall ritual anyway and create a feeling of autumn even if she couldn't experience the real thing. Patty was excited about the idea, and her resourcefulness surprised even me. She called friends in Vermont and asked them to send her a box of fall leaves, pine cones, and fresh-picked apples for her ritual. She asked other friends to send photographs of their back-yards, the woods, the lakes, all showing the beautiful oranges, yellows, and reds of autumn. To prepare her nieces and nephews, who of course had no idea what "fall" meant or looked like, she took out books from the library that not only depicted fall but explained why the leaves changed. Soon the kids, who ranged in age from four to four-teen, were as excited about the ritual as Patty.

Together, the family decorated their patio with orange, yellow, red, and brown crepe paper. On large pieces of newsprint, the children drew pictures of trees and pasted on them the real autumn leaves that Patty had imported from Vermont. They put up the photographs as well, creating an autumn oasis in the middle of the desert! For their ancestor's house, they broke down an old orange crate (which are plentiful in Arizona), and refashioned the slats of wood into a little ranch house. The kids painted it, and Grandma supplied pictures of relatives from the old country for its inside walls. Family and friends from all over the state came to participate in the ritual, and all were thrilled to acknowledge the coming of autumn, Northern style! Patty tells me that everyone had such a good time, they all left saying they'd be back, same time next year.

When my friends Ann and Stuart moved from New York City to Massachusetts with their two daughters, they created a tailor-made fall holiday. The changing seasons had become a more important issue in their lives, because they spent more time together in nature. Also, gardening, a new endeavor for the family, made them pay attention to the best growing times. Stuart was brought up in the Jewish faith, while Ann was raised as a Christian, and they wanted to celebrate an inclusive holiday with their children, honor-ing both their religions and seasonal change. Hence, Ann and Stuart created what they call "Seasonfest," a ritual for all seasons that incor-porates old-time family traditions as well as newer beliefs that the couple shares.

Seasonfest takes place at the beginning of autumn, winter, spring, and summer, and the intention is to honor the family's relationship with nature and their respect for all types of spirituality. Ann and Stuart always try to pick a day in the early part of each season—a day that smacks of that time of year: the crispness of autumn, a dark winter day with snow on the ground, a balmy spring day amid the trees in bud, a June day bursting with the promise of summer. Whenever possible, they do this ritual outside. Sometimes they go to a clearing in the woods or a park; other times they stay in their own backyard. Their "summerfest" celebration is often held by the ocean or near a lake. In inclement weather, they bring into the house whatever symbolic items speak of the season they're honoring—autumn leaves, summer flowers, a winter icicle, a spring bud.

The family often invites other families to celebrate with them. Their rituals always begin by creating a circle and having everyone hold hands. Each person has a chance to speak about the season. The words might be a prayer, a thank you, a description of the season to come, a short poem, a quote someone found in a magazine, a picture someone else painted, a memento from a vacation, or simply ideas about what an individual plans to do or what he or she likes about that season. People can say whatever pops in their minds or come prepared with a poem, a song, or a dance.

Ann and Stuart now do this ritual four times a year, each time allowing for spontaneity. Some of their Seasonfests have been mostly conversation, while others have featured a great deal of singing and dancing. Every time they do this ritual, they get slightly different results, but they always ring in the new season with style. Best of all, this family has created an enduring tradition that embodies their beliefs and their connection to Mother Earth.

8. Acknowledging Hard Times

EVERY FAMILY goes through hard times—illness, death, financial difficulties, anxieties about a new school or a new job, separation, or divorce. Although change is an inevitable part of life, it is hard on everyone, particularly when new circumstances seem strange, difficult, or downright bad. Still, we must learn how to accept these challenges and teach our children how to cope with them as well. Indeed, for kids to grow into conscious and mature adults, they need to experience the bitter times with the sweet.

Many of us tend to suppress our emotions during these rocky passages. Some believe that emotions are dangerous and that we should move quickly beyond them. Others think that if we don't express the bad feelings, they will just go away. Even worse, in the last decade, some people have suggested that being spiritual means that rather than experiencing bad feelings, you immediately transmute all negativity into bliss.

But in disowning the full range of our feelings, we're ultimately left feeling empty—and unable to cope. "We have undergone some sort of emotional lobotomy," maintains Ngakpa Chogyam, an English-born Buddhist lama, author of *Rainbow of Liberated Energy,* "in which all we have gained is the dubious and vaguely arid comfort of feeling in control of the situation."

The truth is, denied feelings inevitably come back to haunt us, or they emerge in other ways. The child who doesn't process his fear of starting kindergarten starts having nightmares. The teenager who can't express his doubts about the new social scene in junior high school becomes withdrawn. The husband who is worried about finances but fails to admit this to his wife ends up barking at her for no reason. The divorced woman who tries to function as if nothing happened eventually falls ill because she has never taken the time to process her ex-husband's abandonment or the failed marriage.

However, we can teach our children and ourselves not to judge our feelings, but instead to accept them, express them, and then move on. Anger, pain, and sorrow are healthy if we feel them and then release them. It is the attachment to negativity, *not the feelings,* that creates problems and isolation. On the contrary, by dealing with our emotions in the moment rather than suppressing or ignoring them, we create a healthier environment in which everyone thrives. We not only promote physical and emotional health, we also give our children a gift that will last a lifetime. In teaching them to honor their feelings, we help them begin to see emotions as guideposts that help them navigate the uncertainties of life. The rituals of change in this chapter give children tools to weather tough times and send a powerful message to every member of the family: You can handle whatever happens in life, without being afraid of your feelings.

Expressing Anger

OF ALL THE EMOTIONS that people find difficult to express, anger ranks the highest. Some people, women and girls especially, have been conditioned to believe it's not "nice" to express anger. They hold in their rage, often turning it against themselves. Repressed anger breeds sickness and turns the person into a time bomb waiting to explode. At the opposite extreme are those who let their emotions build up and allow old anger and resentment to reach the point of rage. We all know such people; they explode over seemingly insignificant incidents, and we wonder what got into them. Research shows that anger can be particularly dangerous to children; those who are prone to rage often have serious behavioral problems later in life, and kids who can't deal with strong emotions tend to feel out of control. Therefore, it's important to help children express anger in healthy ways—and the earlier they do, the better they'll make their way in the world.

Healthy anger is released at the time it happens and is expressed appropriately. Ancient cultures recognized the importance of learning to feel and release rage. The Mayans used a water ritual to release negative and angry feelings. They shouted their feelings into a rushing brook or another body of water, which carried the emotions downstream and out of their lives. Another anger ritual involves making a male figure, whom Mexicans call "Dr. Gloom," out of papier-mâché. People then write down their problems on pieces of paper, place them on the statue, and then set it on fire. And the Chippewa Indians still conduct a ritual in which people go into the woods, dig a hole, and pour their feelings into the earth. They then pray that their problems will transform into fertilizer to nourish the Earth Mother.

This ritual is a combination of old-time ritual and modern-day psychology that encourages people to "get their feelings out." It is particularly important for children, because it acknowledge that it's acceptable to vent anger and gives them a tool to do it.

Making an Anger Mask: You can make an anger mask either during Family Meeting time or as part of this ritual, although the latter might be difficult if the person is really angry. Cut a plain mask out of cardboard (or if you're really ambitious, make one out of papier-mâché), leaving holes for the eyes, nose, and mouth, or buy a plain paper or plastic mask, which can be purchased at any craft store. Use quick-drying paints suited to the surface of the mask you make or buy. The idea is to paint this plain mask in colors and designs that symbolize the anger of who-

ever is making it—stars or zigzag designs or whatever pattern expresses that person's feelings. If you're doing this with children, put down plenty of newspapers so they can be rough and sloppy.

Recipe: When you feel yourself or your children becoming angry, instead of trying to calm them or yourself down, encourage expression of these feelings by having the angry individual put on an anger mask and vent. Shout, cry, pound the pillow, or make a racket by banging the drum or even just hitting the sticks together. Engage in a screaming contest or see who can make the most noise. If you live in an apartment, you might want to play music so the neighbors don't call the police! Or, go outside to a deserted park or near a lake or river where no one will bother you.

Releasing emotions in this way eventually leads to a quieting of the inner turmoil. After a while, the anger will become more subdued and exhaustion will set in. The angry person then removes the mask and sits down. Cleanse the space by burning the sage in a fireproof bowl. Place some melissa in the small muslin bag to hang around your (or the angry person's) neck. According to aromatherapist Scott Cunningham, this scent makes its bearer "beloved and agreeable."

Finally, write a list of all the things that made

you angry. Rip up the list and burn it in the fire-proof bowl, symbolically releasing the negativity. Repeat aloud: "With this ritual I express and release all that angers me at this moment. I promise myself I will not withhold my anger."

Follow – Up: Keep the anger mask (or masks, if several family members have made them) in a special drawer or closet where the mask can easily be found. The next time someone is angry, repeat the above ritual.

RITUAL REALITIES: Parents I know have used a number of approaches to deal with their family's anger.

ℯ Nate, a film executive in California, had a tendency toward irrational rages—a hair-trigger response he inherited from his own father. When his son, Michael, was born, he, too, seemed prone to tantrums. Determined to change the old pattern, a few years ago Nate started doing my anger ritual with six-year-old Michael. Whenever either of them feels angry, father and son play their "anger game." They put on their masks for a few minutes and make menacing noises at one another, which eventually turn into laughter. Sometimes, they also get into the car and drive around Beverly Hills with the windows up, each trying to outshout the other. Their screaming contests also invariably cause father and son to start laughing. Afterward, they go out for ice cream—a sweet way to end their anger ritual.

ℯ The Worthington family—Mom, Dad, teenager Chris, and ten-year-old Megan—used padded moving blankets and huge pillows to create a damage-proof area in a portion of their basement rec room, turning it into "the anger corner." Whenever anyone feels angry, she can ask to use the anger corner. Or, sometimes, someone suggests that another family member uses it. The person is allowed to scream, bang, pound, even curse, as long as she contains her rage in that little corner.

ℯ Jane was worried because her five-year-old daughter, Daria, seemed to lose control so often. Because Daria was a good artist and loved to draw, Jane suggested making a picture book about a little girl named "Dora" who got mad at everyone and everything. In her drawings, Daria showed the fictional Dora getting into trouble. Dora hit playmates when she didn't like the way they played a game. Dora grabbed toys from other kids. Seeing Daria's pictures gave Jane a better understanding about her daughter's anger. And having a safe way to talk about anger—Dora's anger—helped Daria release some of her own feelings. It also helped mother and daughter avert angry clashes *before* they happened.

᨝ *Healing a Rift*

FIGHTS ARE INEVITABLE in families. Older siblings get angry at younger ones for invading their turf. Younger brothers and sisters rage about being left out or picked on. And they all get angry at parents! A reminder to do homework, a request to help with a chore, misplaced items, misunderstood sentences—anything can send a child into a tantrum. Doors slam, children hide, parents groan—and everyone needs a time-out, if not a vacation. Psychologists insist that such blow-ups are "good" for families, in that they can clear the air and ultimately bring everyone closer. The question is, when one person believes he is "right" and the other feels wronged, how do we move from experiencing distance and hurt to making peace?

In olden times, churches and temples were central places of refuge where people went to talk to a clergyman without fear of reprisal or to pray for healing and redemption. Many cultures also performed special rituals to heal conflicts. In some African communities, for example, a safe space was created by inviting an enemy to eat. No one could be considered an enemy after sharing food, which in many societies today is still a central element of peacemaking. Similarly, the ancient Hawaiians had a *pu'uhonua* ("place of refuge")—a sanctuary in which a priest performed a purification ritual. Once cleansed, anyone who had been to a *pu'uhonua* could safely return to normal life, past crimes forgotten. No one could retaliate against or demand retribution from the person, not even the highest chief. The rules of this powerful ritual even applied to people who were about to be put to death for their crimes and to soldiers from defeated armies. All were spared if they could reach a *pu'uhonua* before being captured.

In our families today, we also need to create our own safe places that allow individuals to heal at their own pace. The following ritual embraces the spirit of *pu'uhonua* and other ancient rites that fostered peaceful conflict resolution.

Intention: To create a safe space for healing.

Timing: After any kind of emotional altercation or out-and-out fight between family members.

Ingredients: A peace dove for each family member (see below), fluorite crystal (absorbs negativity), bergamot or chamomile oil (peace) or crushed flowers in water, pen and pad or tape recorder, "Help" sign (see below), matches, pink candle (compassion), salt water in a bowl, and a piece of bread (making peace), symbol of hatchet (conflict).

Making Peace Doves: Each person creates a dove, either out of clay or by framing a drawing or magazine cutout of a dove pasted onto cardboard. Everyone labels the dove with his or her name and leaves it on the family peace altar (see recipe).

Making a "Help" Sign: Bend half of a three-by-five-inch index card in half again, making it into a little tent. Using magic marker or pen, write the word "Help!" on both sides. Keep near family altar.

Recipe: Designate a certain place in your home for the peace altar. Keep everyone's doves on the altar turned around with their backs facing the room. Place a fluorite crystal on the altar, too, as well as some bergamot or chamomile oil, or crushed flowers in water. If it's possible to have a "dedicated" tape recorder for this purpose, keep it near the altar, or simply leave a pad and pen nearby.

Explain that when a rift occurs, the injured party or parties will write down all their feelings or talk them into the tape recorder, releasing all the bad feelings. The comments should be directed at the particular family member or members involved in the rift, but "I" statements should be encouraged: "I feel angry because you wouldn't let me go to the party," "I feel hurt that you ignored me," or "I feel bad that you kicked me out of your room," instead of, "You are being unfair," "You made me feel bad," or "You're mean." Small children may need parents' assistance. For example, if your three-year-old looks angry, help her get started by asking about her feelings: "You look angry. Is something making you feel bad inside?" Instead of talking or writing, young children can draw their feelings.

The person then places the tape, letter, or drawing on the altar, and turns her dove around, facing forward, to let the other person(s) know she wants to make peace. If she feels she needs a mediator—say, a younger sibling is angry at an older one—she should place the "Help" sign next to the dove.

When the other person involved in the rift sees the dove turned around, he reads the note, looks at the picture, or listens to the tape, and places his version of the argument on another piece of paper or tape. He then turns his dove around, too. At an agreed upon time, both parties will meet at the altar.

Although it is possible for older children to come together on their own, when your family first starts practicing this ritual, it's a good idea to make it part of a Family Meeting in which both parties can be heard. The two people sit together in front of the altar and light a pink candle to symbolize that they are ready to make peace. Remember this is a safe space—no blaming is allowed. Each person has a chance to express his feelings, but no one is allowed to attack the other. No one should take sides either. This is not about proving anyone right or wrong. The idea is to be heard.

After their respective grievances have been aired, with the rest of the family bearing witness, the parties wash their hands in the salt water as a sign of release and purification. Together, they also break the piece of bread as a sign that they are no longer "enemies." If possible, have the parties go outside and literally bury the hatchet (or a symbol of it—a piece of wood, a rock, or a piece of paper with a hatchet drawn on it).

Follow-Up: How often we joke, "Oh, we ought to have a tape of this argument since it comes up so often!" Well, in this case, you will have tapes or at least notes of past disagreements, and it may break the ice to bring them out when "the same old issue" comes up. The purpose of revisiting the past is not to say, "See, you always do this," but rather to thoughtfully assess family patterns. When you begin to recognize that a particular kind of quarrel or misunderstanding recurs, add another component to this ritual: a brainstorming session about what everyone has learned from the argument and what you can do differently to avoid a battle in the future. Be aware, however, that *arguments are a part of family life.* You won't obliterate conflict; but you will help everyone know how to deal with it more effectively.

RITUAL REALITY: Single mother Olivia was desperate when she called about her sons, Jason and Jeremy, twelve and thirteen. The brothers were only eleven months apart, and the older they grew, the more they seemed to battle at home over their respective turf. Olivia felt more like a referee than a mother. I suggested that she extricate herself from the boys' battles by setting up a family peace altar and teaching them this ritual. She was more than skeptical. At first, her boys laughed at the idea of any kind of altar in the house. "What is this, church?" scoffed Jeremy. But Olivia held her ground, and she sat down with the boys one afternoon and all of them made little doves out of Play-Doh. "This is stupid," Jason said later that night. "Jeremy's never going to go along with it." Olivia simply said, "We'll see."

The next evening Jason was in tears. "Jeremy called me a 'dork,' Mom," he complained.

"Well, you know what to do," Olivia answered, pointing to the peace altar.

Jason shrugged, made a face, and said, "Yeah, right." Still, he did what his mom had suggested, and wrote in the notebook she had left on the altar: *I feel embarrassed and stupid when Jeremy calls me a dork. I think that I can't do things as good as him. I feel lonely when he slams the door in my face.* Then, he turned his dove around to face the room. Next to it, he placed the "Help" sign.

Just in case Jeremy didn't think to check the altar, Olivia gently reminded him. To her amazement, he did his part of the ritual, too. The boys agreed to meet the next evening. They asked Mom to be there, too. This healing ritual worked for two reasons—it gave the boys a chance to vent their feelings *and* time to cool off. The next evening when they met, each boy listened patiently as the other read his list of feelings. "I'm sorry, Jason," Jeremy volunteered after listening to his brother. "I didn't realize you felt so bad."

"Me, too, Jeremy," added Jason. "I didn't know that all my questions were annoying you so much and that's why you got mad at me."

Afterward, the boys buried a toy hatchet in the backyard. Naturally, this wasn't their last argument—far from it. But at least they began to get into the habit of expressing their feelings and, just as important, listening to and respecting each other's point of view.

Divorcing Parents' Commitment Ceremony

AS I EXPLAINED in my first book, *The Joy of Ritual,* there are few rituals for families going through divorce, especially where children are concerned. Many times, the adults' pain and anger inhibits their ability to see their children's reactions clearly. They become so self-involved, they fail to address kids' anxieties and concerns or answer their questions. However, parents must keep their eyes open. If their feelings and fears are not attended to, children tend to blame themselves for the breakup and feel that their family has been ripped apart.

Of course, there are no precedents for this in earlier societies. Divorce is a relatively new cultural phenomenon. At least, many conscious parents explain to their children that the decision to divorce is an adult one, that it is not the kids' fault, and that Mom and Dad will still be their parents (albeit from different houses). Still, it is important to create a ceremony that honors this tumultuous family transition. In my first book, I offered two types of divorce rituals, one that is done with the divorcing partner, another that is done alone. This ritual is designed specifically to be done with the kids. I call it a "commitment ceremony" because it reaffirms parents' undying dedication to their children—literally, till death do they part. "Divorce ends a marriage—it does not end a family," writes divorced parent Melinda Blau in *Families Apart: Ten Keys to Successful Coparenting.* "[Coparenting] is the least we can do for our kids. After all, *we* broke the contract. Our kids were *supposed* to have two parents—divorce or no divorce."

Intention: To reassure the kids that not being married doesn't mean losing either Mom or Dad.
Timing: As soon as possible after one parent moves out of the house.
Ingredients: Matches, white candle

(the past), something bitter (horseradish), something sweet (honey, chocolate, sweet wine), wedding rings, a key on a cord (one from each parent, one for each child), blue candle (the future).

Recipe: Have the whole family come together in a neutral space. If you can, pick a place in nature where you all feel comfortable. If you must do this ritual inside, don't use either parents' home, especially if there are lingering resentments about having to move out. Before the ritual, the divorcing partners should prepare a list in advance of what they appreciate about the marriage and each other. For example, "I'm grateful that this marriage produced two wonderful children" or "I'm thankful for the support you gave me in my career." Be sure each point is well thought out, focusing especially on the positive.

Begin by lighting the white candle, explaining that it represents the past. Everyone should take a few deep breaths and do a short, relaxing meditation (see page 29). Then, each parent briefly shares his or her list, speaking in clear and simple terms. Children need to learn that life has its ups and downs, that circumstances change, but that they had nothing to do with the separation of their parents. As everyone takes a taste of something bitter and something sweet, explain to the children, "This is a reminder that life includes both joy and sorrow. We all must learn to embrace both kinds of experience to live life fully."

The parents then take off their wedding rings and place them in a box. The rings can either be given to the children or you can bury them or throw them out. (Decide this in advance by gauging your children's reaction; some may be upset by the idea of discarding the rings altogether.)

Both parents now hold their children's hands and say their own version of, "You are the gift of our union. Now it is time for our family to change its form and for all of us to move on to a new phase of our lives. Although we will no longer live together as a husband and wife, we are still your parents, and we hereby make this commitment to you, to be the best parents we can."

Each parent then recites a personal vow to the child and offers a copy of each statement so that each child can keep and refer to these vows in the future. You can make these up, as you would the vows for a wedding ceremony, or use something along these lines: "I, Joe, promise to love and take care of you. Through times of anger, fear, or any other difficulties, I will always keep my heart open. I will always be your father." After reciting the vow, the parent gives each child a symbolic key to their heart. (It can also be a key to the parent's new home.) The other parent repeats the same sequence. Finally, light the blue candle as a symbol of closure and the promise of a new relationship.

Be prepared for tears. This is a bittersweet ceremony and may be difficult for all involved. It will, however, set the intention for a healthy relationship within the new family unit.

Follow-Up: Try to maintain as many of the old routines as possible and stick to your commitment to spend time alone with your children. Remember, too, that divorce is not an event; it's a process. Allow time for a child to absorb the shock of so many changes. In the months that follow, reminisce about the commitment ceremony and ask your children if they feel you're sticking to your vows. Keep the lines of communication open, because as children get older they begin to understand more. They often have more questions about the divorce, the new living arrangements, the schedule, or just want to talk about their own feelings. No matter how painful it is for parents, they need to make the time and space for this expression of feelings.

RITUAL REALITY: The Petersons are not necessarily representative of most divorcing couples, but their story is certainly inspirational. Bob and Margery, both city clerks, had been married for twelve years when Bob asked for a divorce. At first Margery flew into a rage; her white-picket-fence dreams were shattered and, even worse, she worried about the effects of the separation on their two children, Collin and Zoey, then six and nine. At Zoey's teacher's suggestion, the couple sought the help of a family therapist, and they went for joint sessions for a good three months before they told the children about their decision and Bob's moving out. Though she was still angry, therapy helped Margery deal with the fact that their marriage was not perfect. She also knew that Bob loved the children as much as she did, and she wanted to make the transition as easy as possible for everyone. So, she put her own anger aside. "If I couldn't have the best marriage in the world," she told me, "at least I could have a good divorce."

Margery and Bob talked to their therapist about what, when, and how to tell the kids about their separation. After choosing Bob's moving-out day, they asked me if I'd do a parental commitment ceremony for them on that day. It was my first. I asked each of them to write their vows to the children.

On the day of the ceremony, I was shocked to

find the house filled with friends and family, including both sets of grandparents. "Right from the start, we want everyone to know that we're going to share parenting," explained Bob when he saw the surprised look on my face, "and we thought making this a community event was a good way of driving the point home." Indeed, they did. And although the children were definitely sad to see their father pack his bags, realizing that everyone supported the new family arrangement made the change a bit easier to bear.

~ Mourning a Loved One

BECAUSE THE DEATH of a loved one is always quite painful, adults often try to shield children from the experience. Sometimes we don't allow them to go to funerals. Afterward, we find it difficult to talk about the deceased without getting emotional, and we fear that our sadness will frighten the kids. In fact, we often feel unable to cope with our own sense of loss, let alone discuss death with a child. However, as we pass through Elisabeth Kübler-Ross's well-known stages of death and dying—denial and isolation, anger, bargaining, depression, and, finally, acceptance—we cannot leave our children alone to go through this process.

Ancient cultures knew the importance of helping even the youngest members of the tribe or community experience loss. Even in other modern cultures, such as in Africa, children are not separated from death as they are in the West. Many places perform elaborate prayer rituals, some of which go on for days and weeks, involving dancing and costumes; typically, every member of the extended family participates. The fact that children are allowed to participate and witness mourning as a natural part of the process gives them a greater understanding of the cycles of life. Many cultures also have specific customs around death: Observant Jewish men do not cut their hair or shave during the mourning period; Chinese mourners must wear a simple robe made out of a burlaplike material; Greek and Italian women still wear "widow's black" for a year. And tribes throughout the world paint their bodies and cover themselves with mud and ashes to symbolize death.

Though they may not cry and carry on the way we adults do, our children are deeply touched by death. They need the time and space to grieve, both because they will feel the absence of that person and also because they need to learn that death is a part of life. As Dr. William Kroen points out in *Helping Children Cope with the Loss of a Loved One,* "... when we can help our children heal the pain of the deepest emotional wounds—the death of a loved one—we are giving them important skills and understandings that will serve them the rest of their lives."

Loss can be sad, often wrenching, but death in and of itself is not morbid—and it's not something we need to shield from children. We all must learn to accept death as a part of life. Learning how to cope with these feelings and to carry on with one's life are essential to a child's well-being. Talking to children about death also allays their fears of something happening to you or them. For example, it's a good idea to reassure a young child that Grandma did not die of the same sore throat she has, or that Uncle Charlie did not die because he drove at night. And it doesn't hurt to let kids know that you are healthy and they are safe. Remember, too, that children grieve in spurts because they can't sustain emotions for extended periods. This ritual of remembrance can help them mourn over time and at their own pace.

Intention: To remember and honor the dear departed who have made our lives meaningful.

Timing: Any time you're feeling the loss is appropriate, but most people conduct this ritual on the birthday of a loved one or the anniversary of his or her death.

Ingredients: Small table, picture of the deceased, lilies (connection to Spirit), essential oil of lavender (accessing grief), diffuser, matches, white candle (Jewish mourners light a *yarzheit* candle, available in most supermarkets, on the anniversary of a loved one's death), music (the loved one's favorite or something that reminds you of that person), symbolic items to share with deceased (see Recipe for explanation), the loved one's favorite foods.

Recipe: The size of the gathering is optional—the immediate family or members of your extended clan as well as close friends who knew the deceased. Explain that you will come together for an evening or afternoon and ask the participants to bring symbolic items representing what they've done the previous year, bits of news and accomplishments that they would have liked to share with the person if he or she were still alive. Children may bring pictures they drew, tests or papers on which that they got good grades, favorite dolls or toys, cookies they baked. Adults might choose to share pictures of a new spouse or grandchild, a medal, a business card indicating success. Have the loved one's favorite foods on hand.

Set up a small table in the middle of the room, making an altar with a picture of the deceased and the lilies. Have everyone gather around the table. Place some lavender oil in a diffuser. Begin by lighting the white candle in remembrance of the deceased. Have everyone join hands and then take a moment of silence or say a prayer aloud. Play the loved one's favorite music, or join voices in a hymn such as "Amazing Grace."

One at a time, each person stands and brings to the altar the item that they would like to give the deceased, explaining its significance. For example, Mark might bring a scrapbook of his trip to Greece, Carla a sweater she finally finished knitting, Kevin a prize won at school. Encourage everyone also to share their favorite stories about the loved one. This is a time for remembering and celebrating the person's life and spirit. It is also a time for tears. Don't be afraid to show your feelings of loss in front of your children.

To end the ritual, share the loved one's favorite foods—Grandma's favorite chocolate cake, Uncle Charlie's special chili, cousin Susan's banana bread. Such delectables can bring up wonderful memories of the deceased. Don't be shy about sharing memories of times your loved one ate these particular dishes.

Follow-Up: Doing this ritual annually will produce amazingly different results, as children get older, and as you all put more distance between yourselves and the person's passing. As children get older, they might want to talk about traits they (or you) have in common with the deceased. Milly has Grandpa's green thumb, Warren his sense of humor.

RITUAL REALITY: If we allow them, children can be amazingly creative about rituals and surprisingly comfortable with deep emotions. Jason's mother, Sally, always had encouraged him to talk about his dad, Jim, who died two months before Jason was born. Jason had grown up seeing pictures of his father and hearing stories about his life. But when Jason was six, Sally realized that her son seemed to be feeling his father's absence in a different way. This is not unusual; a child at six experiences death and loss far differently from a younger child. Since Jim's birthday was coming up, Sally encouraged Jason to create his own way to celebrate his father's memory, and believe it or not, he actually came up with this ritual of remembrance (which, I admit, inspired my own!):

On the day of his father's birthday, Jason asked his mother and his two aunts, Judy and Nancy (his father's sisters), to come to his house for "Jim's Day." Jason dressed up in his best outfit—his father's tie, his Little League hat, and cowboy boots because he thought they were grown-up. He placed a photo of his father on the living room coffee table, and surrounded it with all the important things that had happened to him that year—all the things that had meaning for him: baseball cards, his favorite mystery books, his first report card.

In the presence of the three women, Jason began to talk to his dad and to play the piano for him. "Dad, you and I are really alike," he said to Jim's photo. "I play soccer and baseball just like you. Look at my report card. I did really good." He then read a letter he had written for his father.

Dear Dad,

It's too bad you couldn't live to see me. I'm sure you would have made a wonderful father. The rest of the family is doing fine. You picked a great wife, who's the best mom in the whole world. We went to Jekyl and Hyde, a scary restaurant, for dinner. I'm going to sleep-away camp for the first time this year. I know I'm going to have a great time. Love you.

Love,
Your son, Jason.

Finally, he said, "Dad, I hope you are proud of me. I know you only stayed around here for a short while, and that's okay, but I really wish you could have stayed a little longer to be with me." He then turned to his mother, Aunt Nancy, and Aunt Judy and asked them to tell Jim stories. Needless to say, tears were plentiful that day. Jason, who is now ten, has since done a version of this ritual every year, each year wearing a different costume and adding a new twist to his ritual. Last year, for instance, he dressed in a long cape and asked everyone to bring his father's favorite foods.

～ Loss of a Pet

THE LOSS of a pet can be one of the most traumatic events in our lives—harder in some ways than the death of a person, according to psychologist Wallace Sife, who has written a book on the subject. "The grief may be more pronounced," he explained to a *New York Times* reporter. "People open up to pets in a way they don't even to a spouse."

And no wonder: Pets offer us unconditional love. They can be confidants, friends, and companions. Some of us talk about our pets as if they were siblings, children, or mates. In many cases, we treat our pets better than we treat ourselves. And children have a special bond with pets, able to experience an almost symbiotic closeness with their animals. Whether you or your child loses a goldfish, a dog, a cat, a horse, or the robin that comes every morning to feed in your backyard tree, a pet's death is a huge loss—of life, of friendship, of a living spirit that must be mourned.

Pet cemeteries can be found all over the United States, but we are neither the first nor the only culture to revere domesticated animals. Remains of mummified pets have been found from ancient Egypt. In Indonesia, elaborate cremation rites are still performed when a cat dies, because cats are believed to be highly evolved spirits. And now, thanks to the technological revolution, people can log on to the Internet and collectively mourn a pet's passing with millions of other cyber-grievers. Among others, Dr. Sife's new Web site for pet mourners (the Association for Pet Loss and Bereavement, or aplb.org), offers a bibliography of resources, a chat room, counseling, and even a memorial registry for the dearly departed.

Many non–animal lovers scoff at the notion of grieving for a pet, saying, "It's only an animal." Such sentiments show disrespect for both you and the animal kingdom. Do not let their insensitivity stop you from mourning in an appropriate way. If you find a dead goldfish in the bowl and mindlessly flush it down the toilet, it not only cheats your children out of saying good-bye to a beloved pet; it also keeps them from learning about and accepting the cycles of life and death.

Naturally, your child will have many questions—questions that will come up with any death. Where did Lassie go? Is she with God? Is there life after death? Do pets and people go to the same place? All of these are normal and should be answered as simply as possible, according to your personal and religious beliefs. This ritual will help you and your children make time for such questions. It will create a space where family members can come together to share their memories and grief, which will help everyone accept the finality of this sad event.

Intention: To grieve the loss of your pet.
Timing: A few days (or longer) after the pet's death, after the initial shock of the loss has worn off. Judge what's best based on your child's age. Generally, the younger the child, the shorter the time between the actual death and this ritual.
Ingredients: Your pet's favorite toy, a photograph or a drawing (or several) of your pet, cypress oil (comfort and solace from loss), diffuser, matches, purple candle (eternal life), a gift from each child to the pet, bowl of water.

Recipe: Come together as a family. Create an altar with your pet's photograph or several photographs. If you do not have photos, use drawings or a symbol, such as a plastic fish, a feather for a bird, a collar for a dog or cat. Also place the cypress oil in the diffuser and put on the altar and light the purple candle. Sit in a circle around the altar, holding hands. Have everyone inhale the aroma of the cypress to give each one comfort.

Going around the circle, allow each person to say good-bye to the pet in his or her own way. Sometimes children will want to sing to their pet or talk to them. Do not censor what your kids want to do. Let them offer up any gift that they feel will help their pet or bring it comfort. One child might offer the family dog a brand-new tennis ball, another a Milk-Bone treat, or his favorite stuffed animal.

Now pass around the bowl of water. As they hold the bowl, family members should try to imagine sending loving thoughts and prayers into the water. Save this sacred water for your pet's burial.

If possible, bury your pet in the woods, in a pet cemetery, or dispose of the body in a ritual way so everyone feels a sense of completion. In many cities, people have to say good-bye to a pet in a veterinarian's office. If that's the case, at least bury a picture of the pet. Whatever sort of burial you perform, complete the process by pouring the sacred water onto the grave. You can also pour the water into the ground outside, giving it to the earth as a sign of sending your prayers to your pet's spirit.

Follow-Up: Encourage your children to talk about their pet, express their sadness, and cry over the loss. It's important that you all continue to release your grief in the weeks and even months to come. However, it's also not a bad idea to consider changing routines that are painful because of their association with the pet. For example, if you always got up at six to walk your dog, set your alarm for seven instead and do a morning meditation before breakfast. If the children ran home from school to play with Fido, pick them up and together do a new after-school activity.

RITUAL REALITY: Chicagoans John and Debbie Morris and their two children, Sarah and Adam, eleven and thirteen, were devastated over the death of Snoopy, their pet beagle. Granted, he had lived to the ripe old age of seventeen. But he had been an engagement present from John to Debbie and was like their first child. Snoopy had grown up with this family. As is the case with many city dwellers, the Morrises had to put Snoopy to sleep at the vet's office. Although all of them were there when the vet administered the final injection, Snoopy's absence in the days that followed left a gaping hole. The Morrises decided to have a mock burial for Snoopy in their apartment. They made an altar out of Snoopy's dog bed, placing on it several photographs of their beloved pet, his collar, and his favorite squeaky toy. They invited good friends and family who had known their pet over the years, and when everyone was assembled, they lit a memorial candle in his honor. The children then dug a hole in the dirt beneath a fichus plant near the window where Snoopy loved to take naps. In it, they put one of the photos of Snoopy, covered it with dirt, and placed a little sign at the base of the fichus, which said, "Rest in peace, Snoopy. We love you." After the burial ceremony, the Morrises served an array of "dog" food: hot dogs, Devil Dogs, chili dogs, and home-baked cookies in the shape of dog bones, explaining, "What better way to honor Snoopy than with his favorite activity: eating!"

9. Making Transitions

Y OUR TODDLER is finally weaned off the bottle. Your six-year-old has outgrown his training wheels. One child goes off to school for the first time, another graduates. Mom changes jobs, and everyone has to move. Dad gets a promotion, so the family takes an unexpected vacation. An older sibling comes home after studying in Europe. The whole family decides to join a new church.

Changes such as these, which mark beginnings as well as endings, define family life. They might be the by-product of one person's metamorphosis or the consequence of an unforeseen event or a crisis that affects the entire family. They might herald exciting times or fear-provoking situations. In any case, as a result of such changes, everyone in the family will move through a transition period.

How do we cope with the unexpected and idiosyncratic changes of family life? How do we address them, honoring the old and embracing the new? Unlike major life cycle transitions (Chapter 5) or the natural progression of seasons (Chapter 7), few traditions address these modern needs. Many ancient and native cultures didn't experience as much stress around these kinds of changes because they had rituals for all reasons and seasons. People knew their "place," so to speak—where they fit in society and in the infinite scheme of things in the universe. No doubt, when so much of life is preordained by custom, it can also work against creativity and spontaneity, but because of these rituals, people in ancient and native cultures didn't agonize over change the way we often do.

In creating the following rituals, I've borrowed and adapted a bit from other cultures. Mostly, though, I've come up with new kinds of ceremonies and rites to help you through transitions. I can't anticipate the exact changes *your* family members will experience. But I can give you general guidelines that can be used to help your family get through them. Adapt my suggestions as you see fit. Take into consideration your unique situation and how each member of your family is affected by it. It doesn't matter what you do, as long as you honor these times of transition.

❧ Moving

ALTHOUGH LEAVING familiar surroundings can be a time of adventure and excitement, it also can be very painful. When I was fifteen, for example, my family moved to a new home in a neighborhood that was an hour away from the community I'd lived in for nine years. Our new home might as well have been three thousand miles away. The transition period lasted three months because my parents were having a house built, which wasn't ready when the school year began. So we still lived in our old house when I started my sophomore year at a new high school. I felt as if I didn't belong in either neighborhood. It was hard to participate in any social events at the new school or to make friends—I lived too far away. And my old friends were involved in after-school activities, of which I was no longer a part. To say the least, it was a traumatic transition.

I didn't know it then, but a moving ritual might have made that transition easier and more meaningful. Ceremoniously marking such a time of change allows us to grieve the loss and to walk toward new circumstances eagerly and with hope. That's why Irish people held an "American wake" in honor of anyone preparing to make the trip to America some one hundred or more years ago. Similar to a wake that follows a death, it was a time for tears and laughter, because the revelers knew that they probably would never see the person again. The next day the "mourners" would walk him to the ship, which was sometimes as far as sixty miles away from their village.

Other cultures have traditions that celebrate and bless a new home. On Malta, a priest prays inside a new house for seven days before newly-weds are allowed to move in. For centuries, Russians have swept their new homes with rock salt, which they believe releases negative vibrations. American settlers came together to help raise the roof of a new home, expressing their welcome and best wishes for safety and security. The Amish still do this. In India, when a family moves into a new home, they paint images of the sun, the Tree of Life, or parrots over the doorways of the house for protection. And for hundreds of years, Jews the world over have placed a mezuzah (a small cylindrical case containing a scroll of Torah verses) outside the door of a new home. Every time anyone enters or leaves, the person touches his fingers to his lips, then to the mezuzah, and recites a prayer: "May God protect my going out and coming in, now and forever."

Although some of these new-house traditions have been carried to this country, more often such spiritual rituals have been replaced or at least overshadowed by housewarming parties. Although parties and presents are wonderful, we're cheating ourselves if we don't connect with the deeper, symbolic meaning of this important transition. In my first book, I offered a New House Blessing, which is part of this ritual as well. First, though, we must honor the wrenching feelings of leaving the old home, and say good-bye to the familiar; then, in the second part of the ritual, we enter and bless the new space.

Intention: To say good-bye to your old home and to bless the new one.

Timing: *Part One:* approximately a week before moving. *Part Two:* the day of the actual move.

Ingredients: *Part One:* family altar (page 30), symbolic items to leave behind (see Recipe), matches, orange candle (happiness), cypress oil (transition), diffuser or bowl of warm water, keys to the new house on new key rings (one for each member of the family), talking stick (page 42). *Part Two:* new welcome mat (see below), salt (purification), coins (abundance), family altar, topaz (new beginnings), vanilla essence (joy), diffuser or bowl of water, matches, lavender incense (to seal the cleansed space), food and camera.

Making a Welcome Mat: At a Family Meeting prior to the move or a time that you carve out especially for this activity, make a welcome mat for the new home. Cut a rectangle out of one and a half yards heavy artist's canvas, allowing one to two inches extra on the sides for the hem. The finished mat will be approximately thirty-nine by twenty-eight inches. Glue the hem neatly with all-purpose glue. Apply three coats of paint to the top surface, allowing the mat to dry between coats, sanding lightly between applications. Create a pattern for your welcome mat on a piece of paper—it could be symbols of your family or an abstract design—and then copy it onto the surface. Paint the pattern and let it dry. When the paint is dry apply three coats of varnish.

Recipe: Once you've finalized your decision to move, find out as much as possible about the new neighborhood ahead of time, especially if you have young children. Draw maps of the area; have plans or pictures of your new home. If possible, visit beforehand and walk around the community with your children or take public transportation. Get a class list ahead of time and contact other parents with an eye toward making play dates. Check the local YMCA or neighborhood center for town activities and classes.

Include your kids in discussions and planning sessions. Let them begin to think about decorating their new rooms. Whether you're packing your own possessions, or having professionals come in, set aside the items on your family altar if you have one (page 30), and pack these only after you have done Part One of this ritual. Place them in a special box or bag that you can bring with you on the day of the move, rather than having to wait for them to be unloaded from the van. If possible, decide in advance where the altar will be situated in the new house. (It's also a good idea to keep one set of sheets, pillows, and blankets for every bedroom in a clearly marked box which will be last in and first out of the mov-

ing van. Often, moving days are quite long, and getting the beds made at least guarantees a comfortable night's sleep.)

Part One—Saying Good-bye: Although packing for a move inevitably takes several days to a week, as part of this ritual, declare one weekend day (when everyone is at home) "Sorting Day." This is a time for family members to go through their possessions and decide what they want to give away and what they want to bring with them to the new home. Pick one small item that each of you will bury in the backyard, thus leaving behind a trace of yourselves. It could be a comb, a toy, a photo—anything that symbolizes your lives in the old house. Expect some sadness, even anger, to erupt. Encourage children's feelings; validate them by sharing your own.

At the end of the day, find a quiet time to gather together around the family altar or in the living room. Begin by lighting the orange candle to represent the happiness that you all shared in this house. Place a few drops of the cypress oil in your diffuser or in a bowl of warm water and ask God to help you through this transition. Place the new keys and key rings on the family altar and say a simple blessing: "Thank you for our new home. May these keys be blessed with good wishes for our safety and happiness."

Now take time to talk about what you're leaving behind and to say good-bye to the house. Pass the talking stick around and share your feelings about the experience of packing your prized possessions and giving things away. Reminisce about the old house, the neighborhood, the people you're leaving behind. Offer your feelings and thoughts about the impending move.

After everyone has had a chance to share, walk from room to room, saying good-bye and expressing gratitude. You might, for example, thank the kitchen for the great nourishment you had, the family room for the fun and sharing, the bedrooms for comfort and rest. If you live in a house and weather permits, include the outside area, saying good-bye to your backyard, your plants and trees.

Now bury the items each of you has chosen. If you live in an apartment, find a tree or garden nearby, or bury the items beneath a houseplant. Leave that plant behind to welcome in the new occupants. Finally, pack up your family altar.

After your immediate family has finished this phase of the ritual, you might want to invite the neighbors to join you in a good-bye party. Keep it simple—pizza or other take-out food, paper plates, or, even better, ask your neighbors to bring the food. Take lots of pictures to remember this day and all the feelings that came with it.

Part Two—Blessing Your New Home:
On moving day, when you arrive at your new home, place the new welcome mat you created outside the door. If the new residence is a house, walk around the house sprinkling salt to purify and protect your home. If it's an apartment, sprinkle a small amount of salt around the front door. Before you enter your new home for the first time, throw coins inside. This is an old Greek custom that is said to bring you wealth. Also place a bit of salt on the floor of each room and then sweep it out to symbolize sweeping out the old energy and bringing in the new.

As soon as the moving crew leaves, don't rush to unpack. Instead, gather together to set up your family altar. Place the topaz on the altar to symbolize this beginning, and add the essence of vanilla (in a diffuser or drops in a bowl of water) to bring joy into your new home. Carrying the lit lavender incense with you, walk around the house together, blessing each room and allowing the scent to seal in those blessings. Make sure to have a living plant in every room to bring in the energy of regeneration. Go into each bedroom and, together, make the beds. Instead of saying prayers separately on the first night in your home, you might want to say them as a family, thanking God for making the move possible and easy.

RITUAL REALITIES: Understand-
ably, moving rituals vary with different family's situations:

❧ When Ellen and Gary moved from Florida to Wisconsin, they wanted to make the transition as easy as possible for Sheila, age eight, and Dirk, eleven. Although these parents couldn't physically take their children to the new neighborhood ahead of time, they asked the real estate agent to take pictures of every room in the new house. To their surprise, the agent did one better: She included a video of the neighborhood. Ellen and Gary also enlarged a local map of the town and highlighted with a yellow marker where the kids' new school was located, the movie theaters, the park, the video parlor, and other spots they knew would interest the children. By doing this, they could show Sheila and Dirk the various routes they'd take, on foot, bike, or by public transportation. By the time the family actually moved, everyone was somewhat familiar with the new location. Although the kids missed their old friends, Ellen told me, they were surprisingly comfortable in the transition.

❧ When Bertha and Arnie and their three children moved into a new home, they decided to ritualize the pouring of concrete into the new driveway. Each person placed his or her footprints in the wet cement, even Bella, their dog. Years later, after Bella had died, the kids commented that it was reassuring to have Bella's paw print—it reminded them of their loyal friend and of the day they moved.

❧ Many parents try to line up friends for their children *before* a move. Dale, an editor who moved during the summer, made sure that she got an advance class list for her daughter so that she could invite the class to her daughter's birthday party in September. Henry, a radio talk show host and inspirational speaker, took his children to visit their new home at least two or three times before moving from Connecticut to Long Island. He also arranged play dates for his six-year-old so she would already have friends at her new home.

~ First Times

IN THE PROCESS of researching this book, I spoke with many child-rearing experts and professionals who deal with parenting issues. Invariably, all of them stressed the importance of helping a child meet the challenge of "firsts," whether it's a first day at school or at a new school, a first time at sleep-away camp, or the first time a teen is allowed to borrow the family car. Life for a child is a series of firsts. Approaching and conquering these milestones helps nurture your child's self-esteem.

Of course, kids don't corner the market on firsts. We grown-ups have to get through them, too. We not only have to get through our children's first times (remember how hard it was to leave your three-year-old at nursery school?), but we also have our own new experiences to deal with—the first day of a new job, attempting a new skill or hobby, meeting with our neighbors in a tenants' association, or giving our first speech.

How do we help ourselves and our children face these new challenges? The circumstances may be different—a child's first bus trip alone is different from an adult's first dinner alone in a restaurant after a separation—but the universal theme is the same. Such moments are both exciting and terrifying because they're new. Rituals can help us face the unfamiliar by allowing us to acknowledge our fears and embrace the unknown.

In my first book, I did a version of this ritual, which is drawn from the Native American practice of creating a symbolic object that acknowledges special gifts. Its purpose is to empower people as they move through various rites of passage, embark on difficult journeys, or attempt new tasks. The Navajos, for example, made a "medicine shield" for this purpose—a frame made from branches, covered in soft leather or canvas. This shield was viewed as a source of comfort, a protection from fear, and a reminder of the wearer's connection to the sacred.

For centuries, men and women also have imbued articles of clothing with symbolic meaning—judges' robes, prayer shawls, policemen's uniforms, or shamanic headdresses. All the better if a new endeavor comes with a special costume, such as a school blazer or a Cub Scout or Brownie uniform; that sometimes makes a transition easier. We feel different in new clothing, miraculously more powerful and in control. But not all firsts involve new outfits. So why not make an article of clothing—a power shirt—and imbue it with qualities, such as strength and courage, that we need to face each new challenge?

Intention: To help make a transition from the known to the unknown.
Timing: Make the "power shirt" a few days before the first day of school, camp, or work, or before any kind of first-time experience; do the ritual on the day the new activity begins.
Ingredients: Family altar, matches, gold candle (self-confidence), inspiring music (a favorite song or piece, or something that the person finds inspirational), bergamot oil (calming), cotton ball, ginger water (courage), fresh or dried dill (clarity), power shirt (see the following).

Making a Power Shirt: First, take a few minutes to think about the answer to this question: What qualities will be needed in the new role or situation? A child starting school might answer, "concentration" or "courage." One taking the training wheels off her two-wheeler might suggest, "balance." A teenager or adult applying for his first or new job might respond by saying, "confidence." Now, using words or images, decorate the T-shirt or tank top with these sentiments. You might also want to choose an animal for inspiration—a lion for leadership, a bear for courage, an ant for patience, an eagle for perspective, a dog for loyalty, or a dolphin for playfulness.

Recipe: Put the ingredients, including the dill, and the power shirt on your family altar or on a small low table. Have everyone gather round it, and then light the candle. Play the music you have chosen. Place a few drops of the bergamot oil on a cotton ball and inhale. Say, "As we breathe in this aroma, all fears and obstacles will leave the room. We feel peaceful, and we send white light toward [name of person] to protect [him/her] in this new phase of his life."

Ask the person to take several deep, slow breaths and to talk about the unique gifts he possesses that will help him now. If it's a young child, it's a good idea not only to prompt but also to talk about his accomplishments. Have the person take a sip of the ginger water and put on the power shirt. He will absorb all of the qualities it depicts.

Follow–Up: Remind the wearer that whenever she needs a boost of courage, she can wear her power shirt underneath her clothes—it is a mighty talisman.

RITUAL REALITIES: Parents can use power shirts or come up with their own rituals to help children through first-time events:

૯ Because Nathaniel was about to enter kindergarten, and the new schedule meant altering their morning ritual, Vickie, a nurse and a single parent, knew it was important to prepare her four-year-old son for the changes. The power-shirt idea appealed to her. She talked with him about the new routine, and because children need concrete reminders, she also marked the days off on a calendar. About a week before kindergarten was about to begin, she helped Nathaniel make a power shirt. Using a new, soft, white T-shirt and magic markers, Vicki helped Nate draw an eagle on his shirt; he loved birds, and he told his mom he wanted to feel like he could fly.

On the first day of school, Vicki and Nathaniel got up a little earlier to make time for their ritual. Before he got dressed, Vicki lit a vanilla-scented candle in her son's room. She explained that it would bring him joy. The two of them talked about how their new routine would change their mornings; they also talked about their fears. They both held Nate's power shirt and Vicki said, "This shirt will give you courage and protect you." They had a candlelit breakfast together, and Nate boarded the school bus, wearing his power shirt under his school clothes.

૯ On the first day of school, Michelle, an editor of a parenting magazine, always takes a picture of her children—in the same place. If their old T-shirts still fit, she also tries to photograph them in the same clothes. The photos are then kept in a "first-times" album, along with other memorable new experiences.

✐ Last Times

ONE OF THE MOST life-changing courses I ever took was a five-week seminar given by Robert Fritz, author of *Creating*. It taught me that in order to manifest what I wanted in my life, I first had to visualize it . . . as I would like it to be. I later became a teacher. Fritz also taught me the power of completion, stressing how important it is to say "I did it" when you finish something. It is a way of telling your subconscious that you have succeeded. When you acknowledge each achievement, one accomplishment then builds upon the previous one, and before you know it, you're building *a pattern* of success.

As a young adult, I didn't grasp the enormity of acknowledging completions. When I graduated from college, for example, most of my friends and I didn't think it was "cool" to attend the ceremony. Looking back, I realize that I not only cheated my parents and siblings, I cheated myself. Rites of acknowledgment are important.

That's why we're given certificates and diplomas and other concrete tokens of completion. Likewise, when graduates throw their caps into the air at the end of the ceremony, it's a tangible symbol of letting go of the past.

There are many last times in family members' lives—weaning from the breast or bottle, the last nighttime diaper, the last time a child needs a parent to walk her to school, the end of the school year or of camp, the completion of a training program, the last game in a sport season. In our culture, we may go out to dinner to celebrate; at most we take photographs. I think we owe it to ourselves to do something even more enduring.

The following ritual, in which you create a family wall or family tapestry, is my adaptation of a totem pole ritual practiced by the Kwakiutl, the Haida, and the Tlingit, Native Americans of the northwest coast. Each mark on a totem pole commemorates an important accomplishment in tribal history. Instead of a pole, I suggest building a wall of stones, or piecing together a tapestry. Or, you may come up with your own version. No matter how it's built or what it looks like, having a family totem will enable you to mark both small and big milestones, rather than take them for granted.

Intention: To acknowledge an ending or completion and, in doing so, build a pattern for future success and accomplishment.
Timing: Whenever you complete a major event.
Ingredients: Neroli (happiness and joy), diffuser, tape recorder and tape. If you have a backyard: large stones, waterproof paint, brushes, confetti or rice (good luck). If you want to do this indoors: fabric squares, raw cotton canvas about nine by twelve inches, wooden backing for canvas, fabric paint, brushes. Crystal (chosen according to the qualities you want to give to the person). Favorite foods.

Recipe: Begin by gathering the family in a circle (and friends if you think it appropriate for the occasion). Ask the person who completed the event to stand in the center. Place a few drops of the neroli oil in the diffuser. Call for a few minutes of silence, while you all inhale the aroma. With each breath, explain that the idea is to try to deepen your feelings of joy for that person and think of why you are proud of him or her.

After a few minutes, family members take turns holding the tape recorder and speaking into it. They tell the person in the middle what they feel about this accomplishment. Take your time. Encourage the person in the middle to be open to receiving the positive feedback.

When everyone is finished, the person who is being celebrated gets to share what it means to him to have completed this event. Then each person showers him with rice or confetti and shouts, "Congratulations!" (If a young child is the celebrant, you may have to tailor the above part of the ritual to his age, keeping each person's comments short and not asking for much of a verbal response—a big smile on hearing everyone's congratulations speaks volumes about how the child feels.)

The celebrant will paint a stone or a fabric square with her name, the date, and any symbol, poem, saying, or word that represents her accomplishment. When the stone is dry, place it outside to start (or add to) a stone wall. Or, if you're making a family tapestry, glue this piece to the larger canvas.

Finally, give the celebrant a crystal that represents a special quality that he or she demonstrated in completing this task—a quartz for focus, amber for balance, rose quartz for love. End the ritual by sharing a spread of the person's favorite foods.

Follow-Up: For each event, year after year, you will add to the wall or canvas. Your family totem will be an enduring comfort. After all, on the road of life, we all have setbacks, moments when we're sure we can't reach a goal we've set for ourselves. When you or a family member is feeling low, look at the family totem. Whether it is a patchwork quilt, a colorful wall, or any other structure you've made, it will remind you of all your accomplishments. You'll remember that those feats once felt difficult, too.

RITUAL REALITY: Thirteen-year-old Davina, who had been seeing the same reading tutor since second grade, was overjoyed when her tutor, Mrs. Stein, told her she was ready to work on her own. Davina's mother, Sally, who had been to one of my workshops, had already begun a mosaic table composed of painted tiles that represented the various accomplishments of each family member. They called their version of a family totem their "terrific table." The end of five years of weekly tutoring sessions was certainly tile-worthy and a good reason to celebrate.

The family had already come together to commemorate other important milestones and had painted tiles for each of these occasions. When Davina's older brother Rick graduated, they drew a mortarboard and tassel on his tile. For the removal of both kids' braces, there were tiles showing teeth. The kids had drawn pictures representing their last days at camp and school. One tile, a cigarette with a big red line through it, marked the day Sally finally quit smoking, and a sailboat tile represented the time Dad completed a sailing course.

Since Davina was familiar with the ritual, she jumped at the idea of making a tile to symbolize her academic independence. She decided to ask Mrs. Stein to write "Good work!" on her tile. Davina then added a gold star for good measure.

During the ceremony to install Davina's tile, everyone in the family reminisced. Sally recalled how hard it had been for Davina to learn to read but how diligently she then worked to improve herself. Rick said he was proud of his "Little Squirt," as he loved to call Davina. Dad admitted that he once had problems in school, too. He told Davina she was lucky to have such a great tutor, but that Mrs. Stein was also lucky to have such a hardworking pupil. Davina couldn't have been prouder as she glued her tile on the table.

Welcoming a New Family Member

THE MOST PROFOUND family rituals can emerge from a sense of sharing good times and significant events of the past. With second marriages, however, there is no such history, and building one can be difficult. By nature, families are a closed system, and adults and children often have trouble allowing new members to join. This is true whether a remarriage occurs after a divorce or death. Both situations have their inherent difficulties. With the former, exes must be dealt with as well as, in some cases, the residual anger that children feel in their absence. Marrying a widow or widower, new partners must deal with the ghost of a deceased partner.

No wonder these are hard transitions. It's rarely just a matter of welcoming in a stepparent; new siblings often come into the picture as well—kids who may live in the house only part time, which further complicates matters. If the new couple then has a child, children of the first marriage may ask, "Why are they doing things for the new baby that no one did for us when we were born?"

It's not just the children who have a hard time. For example, a stepmother who has children of her own not only has to welcome her new husband's children—and vice versa—but she also must deal with her own children's grief and anger. On the other hand, a stepmother (or father) who is childless has to adjust to the daily drama that living with children entails. Clearly, it takes maturity and flexibility on the adults' part, not to mention creativity and patience, because there are dozens of potential minefields—discipline, money management, the logistics of each person's space, and the many other issues that the new couple has to work out in the face of all this confusion.

Not surprisingly, rituals are often a source of

conflict in these families. Do we cook foods we always did? Or does the new stepmother do things her way? Do the kids spend Saturday mornings watching their favorite cartoons as usual? Or do their new step-siblings change the channel? Do we have Thanksgiving, Christmas, and Easter the way we always did? Or do the new members of the family have their own ideas about these occasions? Ideally, both sides' traditions are honored and in some way combined to create new rituals, but it often takes years to work these things out. In fact, according to Boston University researcher Patricia Papernow, it can take four to seven years—even longer if children are older at the time of remarriage—for a stepfamily to solidify and develop a cohesive sense of history.

I offer no magical prescription to speed up the process. But I do know that it helps to get off on the right foot. Therefore, I have created a welcoming ritual. Based on a traditional Japanese tea ceremony, it can be used to welcome adults or children into the family. To understand its power, you have to know a little bit about the history of this ancient rite which dates back to the twelfth century, when tea was introduced to the Japanese by Zen monks, who brought it from China. The tea ceremony was conceived as an aid to meditation; later, among the nobility, it evolved into an elaborate social rite which prepared a host and his guests to love one another and deepened the harmony between them. Why not adopt it for the new families of today?

Intention: To welcome and integrate new family members.
Timing: After remarriage, when new family members move in—stepparents or stepchildren.
Ingredients: Special tablecloth, geraniums (true friendship), place cards for each person (see below), items that represent your family and the newcomers' possessions, meditation music (a classical piece, new age music, or any kind of chants you enjoy), matches, blue candle (communication), rose incense (love), diffuser or small fireproof bowl, utensils, green tea (with young children, you might want to use flavored herbal tea), tea pot, bowls for tea, optional homemade gifts from each member to the new family member(s).

Making Place Cards: Prior to the ceremony, perhaps in a Family Meeting, take time to make place cards for each member of the family. Make sure each card has a similar unifying element—something as simple as a common last name or a symbol that represents your new family—as well as something unique. For example, if a child is a sports fanatic, his place card might have a baseball on it. If an adult loves to garden, a flowerpot might symbolize that interest.

Recipe: Preparing your home with care is an act of welcome, so take time to make this a special event. Decorate the dining room table with the tablecloth, flowers, and the new place cards. Try to use items that represent the original family (Grandma's tablecloth), as well as the new-comers' possessions (a stepparent's vase). Create a calm atmosphere by turning on the meditation music. Have people remove their shoes. Explain that this is a way to move into sacred space and leave behind the cares of the world.

When everyone is around the table, light the blue candle, explaining that it will symbolically open up communication among family members. Burn the rose incense to open your hearts. Welcome everyone by saying a short prayer or just speaking from your heart. Explain that this is a chance to meet heart to heart and extend a sincere welcome to one another. To do this, you will follow the Way of Tea, principles that were conceived by the great Zen master Sen Rikyu thousands of years ago: harmony, respect, purity, and tranquillity. These are the elements you would like to bring into your new family. You might also want to explain how this ceremony is conducted in Japan.

Traditionally, the host welcomes his or her guests silently, by bowing. The utensils are wiped with a special cloth. Tea, which has been steeping in the teapot, is poured into bowls and set in front of each guest. The bowl is turned halfway around before drinking, which symbolizes a respect for the earth, the potter, the sun, and the tea plant. The guest bows in gratitude for being a part of this ceremony. You might choose to do this ritual as it is done in Japan, but that's not necessary. The important aspect is to create a ritual space in which attention is paid to the idea of sharing and appreciation.

As you share the tea, welcome each member and have each person share his or her thoughts and feelings about being part of this new family. You also might want to give small gifts to one another, ideally homemade items, as another way of saying "welcome." Close the ceremony by holding hands, bowing your heads, and saying a prayer. You can either make one up ahead of time, allow each person to say a short prayer ("thank you, God" is sufficient), or say: "God, we ask you to bless our new family with love, health, and respect for one another. Give us open hearts to welcome one another, strength to get through hard times, and the wisdom to cherish the good times."

Optional: With the popularity of paint-your-own ceramic studios throughout the country, it's possible to make a special tea set for this occasion—a joyful activity in which even the youngest members of the family can participate.

Follow-Up: Use the personalized place cards again and again, for ordinary family dinners and special occasions. Also remember that every occasion, every joint outing, is an opportunity to create traditions and build family history. Cherish those moments and capture them. You might want to begin a photo album or video record of your new family. Make sure that even kids who don't live in the house all the time are included. If you or your kids are artistic, you also might get together and create a family crest. Each person draws (or cuts out a picture) and then you arrange them to form an emblem.

RITUAL REALITIES: Because so many families today are in flux, I can't count the numbers I've counseled about welcoming new members. I've also heard heartening stories from people who have come up with creative ideas of their own. Here is a sampling:

꒰ When they got together, Regina and Carl knew everyone would call their family "the Brady Bunch," since it combined his three daughters, sixteen-year-old Kyra, fourteen-year-old Annie, nine-year-old Kirsty, with her two sons, nine-year-old Bryan and six-year-old Sean. Complicating matters, Carl coparented with his ex-wife Stacy, and the girls spent almost equal time with each parent. Luckily, the adults were on good terms, but Regina, more recently divorced than Carl, hadn't quite worked out the kinks with Slate, her ex-husband. Slate lived three hours away, wasn't particularly cooperative, and saw the boys only once or twice a month. Knowing that they had a difficult road ahead, Regina and Carl sought the help of a counselor to deal with their emotional problems. But they consulted me about Christmas, which came only six weeks after their wedding.

"My kids are used to going skiing—that's what their father and I always did for the holidays," Regina explained. "They resent having to stay home this year. And Slate is too busy with his new girlfriend to take them with him." Carl's daughters were accustomed to being creative around the holidays. His ex-wife was an artist and a great baker, and they recalled a home filled with good smells and strewn with scraps of paper and other materials that they used to make and wrap gifts.

They were angry when their new brothers told them they "weren't into sissy stuff like that."

I suggested that the families think about combining their rituals. Take a day trip or weekend trip around the holidays—teach the girls how to ski. But also take days at home, encouraging the boys to respect their sisters' interest and get them involved in baking and arts and crafts projects as well. Most important, come up with some new traditions, like the tea ceremony. Everyone loved that idea the most, especially the optional part of making a family tea set. Several of the kids had already visited the local paint-your-own pottery shop and enjoyed doing it. As it turned out the kids collaborated on a design for a teapot and they made monogrammed cups to go with it. Of course, the tea ceremony didn't make all the difficulties go away—it took several years to really feel like "family." But the tea set was thereafter used for every special occasion. Most important, it was proudly displayed in the dining room—a reminder of one important step that this Brady Bunch had taken toward creating its own history.

℮ When Margaret started dating Bert, a widower, she was pleased that his daughter, eleven-year-old Gabrielle, warmed up to her so quickly. But as Margaret and Bert became closer and, finally, set a wedding date, she was keenly aware that Gabby might reject her if she thought Margaret was trying to replace her own mother, who had died of cancer three years earlier. A month before the wedding, Margaret took Gabby aside and told her she had a special present for her and that she'd like to take her out to lunch to give it to her. She chose a quiet restaurant Gabby had never been to, in the hope that it would become "their" place. They chatted amiably over candlelight, and then Margaret brought out a beautifully wrapped box. "Gabby, this is for you," she said. "I couldn't think of a better way of thanking you for welcoming me into your family." Gabby cried when she saw the gift. Margaret had asked Bert's mother for pictures of his first wife—Gabby's mom—in the early days of their marriage before Gabby was born, and Margaret had had them framed. "I wanted you to know that I feel like I'm moving in *with* your mother," Margaret added in case there was any question, "not in place of her."

RESOURCES

SUGGESTED READING

Animals

Saunders, Nicholas. *Animal Spirits*. Alexandria, Va.: Time-Life Books, 1995.

Aromatherapy

Cunningham, Scott. *Magical Aromatherapy*. St. Paul, Minn.: Llewellyn Publications, 1996.

Tisserand, Maggie. *Aromatherapy for Women*. Wellingborough, N.Y.: Thorsons Publishers, 1985.

Tisserand, Robert. *Essential Oil Safety Data Manual*. Brighton, Sussex, England: Association of Tisserand Aromatherapists, 1985.

Valnet, Jean, M.D. *The Practice of Aromatherapy*. Rochester, Vt.: Healing Arts Press, 1980, 1989.

Arts and Crafts

Owern, Chery. *Spirit Crafts*. Brighton, Sussex, England: CLB International, 1997.

Terzian, Alexandra M. *The Kids' Multicultural Art Book*. Charlotville, Vt.: Williamson, 1993.

Birth Rituals

Costa, Shu shu. *Lotus Seeds and Lucky Stars*. New York: Simon & Schuster, 1998.

Cards and Oracles

Blair, Nancy. *Amulets of the Goddess: Oracle of Ancient Wisdom*. Oakland, Calif.: Wingbow Press, 1993.

Marashinsky, Amy Sophia, and Hrana Janto. *The Goddess Oracle*. Rockport, Mass.: Element Books, 1997.

Sams, Jamie, and David Carson. *Medicine Cards*. Santa Fe, N.M.: Bear & Company, 1988.

Zerner, Amy, and Monte Farber. *Goddess Guide Me*. New York: Fireside, Simon & Schuster, 1992.

Christian Rituals

Nelson, Gertrud Mueller. *To Dance with God*. New York: Paulist Press, 1986.

Earth Celebrations

Heinberg, Richard. *Celebrate the Solstice*. Wheaton, Ill.: Quest Books, 1993.

Henderson, Helen, and Sue Ellen Thompson. *Holidays, Festivals and Celebrations of the World Dictionary*. Detroit, Mich.: Omnigraphics, 1997.

Ickis, Marguerite. *The Book of Festivals and Holidays*. New York: Dodd, Mead, 1964.

Ingpen, Robert, and Philip Wilkinson. *A Celebration of Customs and Rituals of the World*. New York: Facts on File, 1994.

Johnson, Cait, and Maura Shaw. *Celebrating the Great Mother*. Rochester, Vt.: Destiny Books, 1995.

Kindersley, Anabel, and Barnabas Kindersley. *Children Just Like Me: Celebrations!* New York: DK Publishing, 1997.

———. *Celebrations: Festivals, Carnivals and Feast Days from Around the World*. New York: DK Publishing, 1997.

Moorey, Teresa, and Jane Brideson. *Wheel of the Year*. London, England: Hodder and Stoughton, 1997.

Myers, Robert. *Celebrations—The Complete Book of American Holidays*. New York: Doubleday, 1972.

General Interest

Cahill, Sedonia, and Joshua Halpern. *Ceremonial Circle*. San Francisco: HarperCollins, 1990.

Wall, Kathleen, and Gary Ferguson. *Rites of Passage*. Hillsboro, Oreg.: Beyond Words Publishing, 1998.

NEWSLETTER FOR STAY AT HOME DADS

At-Home Dad
61 Brightwood Ave.
North Andover, Mass. 01845
athomedad@aol.com/www.ath-omedad.com

NEWSLETTER

F.E.M.A.L.E. (Formerly Employed at the Leading Edge)
P.O. Box 31
Elmhurst, Ill. 60126
630-941-3553
www.femalehome.org

Inspirational

Chogyam, Ngakpa. *Rainbow of Liberated Energy: Working with Emotions Though the Colour and Element Symbolism of Tibetan Tantra*. Longmead, England: Element Books, Ltd, 1986.

Kornfield, Jack. *A Path with Heart: A Guide Through the Perils and Promises of Spiritual Life*. New York: Bantam Books, 1993.

Moore, Thomas. *Care of the Soul*. New York: HarperCollins, 1992.

Loss

Brener, Anne. *Mourning & Mitzvah: A Guided Journal for Walking the Mourner's Path Through Grief to Healing*. Woodstock, Vt.: Jewish Lights Publishing, 1993.

Harris, Eleanor L. *Pet Loss*. St. Paul, Minn.: Llewellyn Publications, 1996.

Kroen, William C., Ph.D. *Helping Children Cope with the Loss of a Loved One*. Minneapolis, Minn.: Free Spirit Publishing, 1996.

Meditation

Hanh, Thich Nhat. *The Long Road Turns to Joy: A Guide to Walking Meditation.* Berkeley, Calif.: Parallax Press, 1996.

Men

Bolen, Jean Shinoda, M.D. *Gods in Everyman.* New York: Harper & Row, 1989.

Moore, Robert, and Douglas Gillette. *King, Warrior, Magician, Lover: Rediscovering the Archetypes of the Mature Masculine.* New York: HarperColllins, 1990.

Music

Campbell, Don. *The Mozart Effect.* New York: Avon Books, 1997.

Mythology

Campbell, Joseph, with Bill Moyers. *The Power of Myth,* New York: Anchor Books, 1988.

Parenting

Bettner, Betty Lou, Ph.D., and Amy Lew, Ph.D. *Raising Kids Who Can: Using Family Meetings to Nurture Responsible, Cooperative, Caring, and Happy Children.* New York: Harper Perennial, 1992.

Blau, Melinda. *Families Apart: Ten Keys to Successful Coparenting.* New York: G.P. Putnam's Son, 1993.

Dreikurs, Rudolf, and V. Stoltz. *Children: The Challenge.* New York: Hawthorn Books, 1964.

Rosman, Steven M. *Spiritual Parenting.* Wheaton, Ill.: Quest Books, Theosophical Publishing House, 1994.

Taffel, Ron, Ph.D., with Melinda Blau. *Nurturing Good Children Now.* New York: Golden Books, 1999.

Prayers

Roberts, Elizabeth, and Elias Amidon. *Earth Prayers from Around the World.* San Francisco: HarperCollins, 1991.

Seasonal

Hennes, Donna. *Celestially Auspicious Occasions: Seasons, Cycles, Celebrations.* New York: Perigee Books, 1996.

Imber—Black, Evan, and Janine Roberts. *Rituals for Our Times: Celebrating, Healing, and Changing Our Lives and Our Relationships.* New York: HarperCollins, 1992.

Women

Monaghan, Patricia. *The Goddess Pat.* St. Paul, Minn.: Llewellyn Publications, 1999.

———. *Goddesses and Heroines.* St. Paul, Minn.: Llewellyn Publications, 1998.

Orenstein, Rabbi Debra. *Lifecycles.* Woodstock, Vt.: Jewish Lights Publishing, 1994.

Starck, Marcia. *Women's Medicine Ways.* Freedom, Calif.: The Crossing Press, 1993.

Starck, Marcia, with Gynne Stern. *Cross-Cultural Rites of Passage.* Freedom, Calif.: Crossing Press, 1993.

Walker, Barbara. *Women's Rituals*. San Francisco: Harper and Row, 1990.

SOURCES

APHRODESIA
264 Bleeker Street
New York, N.Y. 10014
Telephone: 212-989-6440
Herbs and oils.

ENFLEURAGE
321 Bleecker Street
New York, N.Y. 10014
Telephone: 212-691-1610
Essential oils, diffusers.

LIFE TREE OILS
3949 Longridge Avenue
Sherman Oaks, Calif. 91423
Telephone: 818-986-0594
Send $2.00 for catalog.
Essential oils, specialty blends.

STICKS, STONES AND BONES
111 Christopher Street
New York, N.Y. 10014
Telephone: 212-807-7024
Incense, charcoal, fireproof
  bowls, crystals, drums, and
  ritual tools.

TSALON
11 East 20th Street
New York, N.Y. 10003
Telephone: 888-NYC-TEAS
www.TSalon.com
Specialty teas.

BARBARA'S FAVORITE MUSIC

Children

Campbell, Don. *Music for The Mozart Effect: Music for Children* (3 volume set). Pickering, Ontario, Canada: Children's Group (800-6668-0242).

Campbell, Don. *Music for The Mozart Effect: Music for Babies, from Playtime to Sleepytime.* Pickering, Ontario, Canada: Children's Group.

Meditation and Birth

Dolphin Dreams (sounds of dolphins, heartbeat, ocean, choir). Boulder, Colo.: Spirit Music.

Meditation/Relaxing

Adorney, John. *Beckoning.* Miami, Fla.: Max Music.

Amma Center of New Mexico. *Amriteswaryai Namaha.* Santa Fe, N.M.: Mahatma Productions.

Anugama. *Healing.*

Coxon, Robert Haig. *The Silent Path.* Canada: RHC Productions.

Demby, Constance. *Sacred Space.*

Kobialka, Daniel. *Timeless Motion.* San Rafael, Calif.: Willow Music.

Lim, Jack. *Inner Peace.* Vic, Australia.

One Hand Clapping: Tibetan Bells with Environmental Sound: Los Angeles: N.O.W. Productions.

World Music

Diop, Wasis. *No Sant.* Triloka Records.

Thornton, Phil, and Hassam Ramzy. *Eternal Egypt.* Suffolk, England: New World Music.

World Music That Speaks to the Spirit (compilation). Triloka Records.